By the Pacific
Poems

Melissa Goldsmith

Melissa Goldsmith
By the Pacific
Poems

MLMC–Gothic and Main
Northampton, MA

What the hell kind of world do we live in—
Hating music, but honoring poetry?
Today and any day,
I want to forget this current world
and take my office to the beach.

This book is for my mother, who loved the Pacific Ocean.
I like to think that somewhere there is a beachside bistro
where Dixieland plays and she can catch
Carradine and Tayback singing together
whenever she wants.

Contents

INTRODUCTION

About four months after I began photography as a hobby, I started writing *Pacific Ocean Poems and Songs*. I became interested in the compact nature of the snapshot: So much can be captured or expressed in a photograph, a tiny piece of space and time in contrast to scholarly or nonfiction writing. Photography may impel people to analyze it, but one cannot deny that the images are also just there—*as is*. One day, this notion of treating the image as it is made me remember my copy of *William Carlos Williams' Selected Poems* and his own approach to poetry. In brief, Williams' approach to writing poems was about focusing on "the thing itself."[1] Both Williams and photography made me wonder if I could apply these notions to writing poetry and if they would help me enjoy writing poetry again.

When I was young, I always loved writing poetry, and perhaps I had some early talent. When I was in elementary school, I was one of several students selected to take poetry classes with a career poet. I recall that as much as he was willing to share his art, he grew increasingly jaded working with inquisitive yet stubborn ten and eleven year olds. Though I always appreciated the opportunity, I remember his displeasure rather than what he taught us. When the classes dissolved, I turned to songwriting and music composition for the first time. Although I wrote music for both school and my own purposes, I began to write poetry generally for school assignments only. By the time I was in college, I was one of few students in my music composition class interested in writing my own song texts. I came to writing my own song texts after leafing through countless poems on topics that appealed to me—but using words and ideas that fell short of what I was hoping for. Between majoring in music and biochemistry, figuring out that I wanted to teach, and working at the library, I fell in love with musicology and writing about music. Composition classes in my program of study were fewer and far between in my graduate years than in my undergraduate ones. I stopped making time for writing poetry.

As a musicologist interested in film and popular music, my interdisciplinary approach to music has always involved a close consideration of the visual image and literature. A film music scholar is expected to be knowledgeable of not only the music and scoring techniques, but also film studies, film editing, aspects of photography, both classical and popular music, song and text relations, cultural and narrative context(s), and musical analysis. Musical, visual, and literary topics are interwoven. Writing poetry, however, stayed on the backburner.

I could have prioritized the creative work; however, as an adult, the idea of writing poetry seemed daunting for several reasons. First, it had been many years since I wrote my last song texts, let alone poems. Second, when I wrote poetry, I recall the

---

[1] Quoted on the back cover of William Carlos Williams' *Selected Poems of William Carlos Williams* (New York: New Directions).

difficulties involved in the writing process. It isn't like when I would write a review or an article, read those pieces some time afterwards, and forget about the effort those pieces required. Somehow, the challenges of making a poem meaningful, caring about its sound, handling the images with words, and working at times with a particular form were all fresher in my mind. Third, I had my own self-imposed poetry writing issues: Whether concrete or abstract, my poems often meant dealing with memory, and truth be told, my memories are not always positive or constructive places to wander. I frustrate easily when one of my poems doesn't measure up to my memories, whether it be the actual topic or the affective content. Most of all, I despise wooden M.F.A. poetry and I still carry a deep fear of producing that kind of rubbish.

Time and photography brought me back to Williams and to writing poetry again. Both photography and Williams' approach to poetry inspired me to stop tangling up images and sounds in my mind before putting them on the page. And if I placed those images thoughtfully in a picture frame or on a piece of paper, those images could be meaningful, even beautiful, just the way they are and in small form. Returning to writing poetry, I began with writing free verse and paying attention to images and sounds. The first poems were brief and aimed at being compact. My concern with their placement took place only while I edited the poems.

Another scholarly avenue I was previously pursuing was exploring the jazz poetry experiments of Kenneth Rexroth, Kenneth Patchen, and Lawrence Lipton, as well as the musicality of poets who did sound recordings, William S. Burroughs, Lawrence Ferlinghetti, Allen Ginsburg, Langston Hughes, John Sinclair, and Jim Morrison. While writing about their sound recordings, I gained exposure to how these poets handled their works as spoken word and as music. While in Thibodaux, Louisiana, a small town on the Louisiana bayou, I became involved on a performance level by reading these poems regularly on a college radio show and planning poetry events known as Beats and Bongos Poetry and Performance Happenings at the local university and a nearby café. Reading these poets aloud led to my own discovery of others, particularly Philip Larkin, William Everson, and jazz poet Bob Kaufman. Personally, if my own poetic voice sounds like any of these poets here, I would like to think that there is something that resembles Williams, Larkin, and Ferlinghetti. At least that is what my ear tells me.

The strongest images that come to my mind come from my childhood spent alongside the Pacific Ocean, mostly in Santa Monica and Santa Barbara, California. With my youngest years spent in Santa Monica as an only child with working parents, I often ended up at the beach, brought there by my mother, a day camp counselor, a babysitter, or by my own two feet. I couldn't have chosen a better couple of cities in which to grow up, especially for my love of the Pacific. Oceans have different colors, temperatures, and waves that make them discernable even when from diverse viewpoints up and down a coast they differ in how they behave or look (for example, it is hard to believe that the calm Pacific with its small waves and lack of undertows in

Carpinteria is the same body of water found in Santa Monica or Big Sur). The Pacific with what I describe here as a turquoise body of water is strikingly different from the Atlantic Ocean that often looks black or dark gray-blue to me.

Pacific Ocean Poems and Songs is a collection of small and large form poems that are composed mostly in free style. There are several pieces with end-rhymes, clear rhythmic and line patterns, structured internal rhymes, and a sense of musical meter, but the poems prioritize images and sounds. Alongside imagery from nature and life on the U.S.'s West Coast, many poems also focus on music, connecting it in various ways to the Pacific Ocean. Some of these poems delve deeply into depression and suicide, whereas others are playfully light, funny, and absurd. At times written from different personas, some poems also focus on characters as well as notable figures who made my home towns their home towns. Two editions of this book exist: One with just the poems themselves and the other with photographs of the Pacific Ocean by Kristina L. A. Schlah. Now living in Northampton, Massachusetts, I asked Kristina if she would provide photographs of the Pacific Ocean. I am grateful that she wanted to be involved in the project, making a gorgeous edition of this collection. I would also like to thank Gothic and Main's Tony Fonseca for helping with the editing process of this collection. *Pacific Ocean Poems and Songs* took about seven months to complete. I believe it is a finished work with poems that are both personable and musical. I've now returned to scholarly writing. If there is a such thing as a muse, she stayed with me for just that long. I fed her well, and she has now moved onto other adventures. I hope we were good for each other.

—*Melissa Goldsmith, 14 March 2015, Northampton, Massachusetts*

Eucalyptus

Lemon-cool impression,
a tree—
Welcomes people
to beachside Western cities
like this one.

Evergreen,
against an
everblue,
an everturquoise,
broken by waves
beyond the reach
of taste.

Just staying
from Australia:
drought-resistant,
highly flammable,
volatile oil—
Ignite by fire, but shade
Palisades Park whinos
in the meantime.

Yate,
young children
adore segmented pods,
white to gray to red bark peelings,
horn-shaped buds,
blooming green to yellow
between nondescript summer
and nondescript winter.
They love your scent,
dreaming well off
into dysfunctional adulthood—
What makes others alert,
makes the natives
calm.

Yate,

4

guilty widow maker
with dense seed cases
and giant boughs,
flail indiscriminately
at unaware pedestrians.
Laugh, growing twisted,
planting
one's foreign roots
into unforgiving,
dusty ground.

Gold Rush relic,
lanky reminder of
get-rich schemes,
opportunist plans—
Fast-growing,
self-motivated,
resourceful roots
that withdraw gold
for themselves.

Cool scent,
smooth bark,
ocean accompaniment—
Align with West Coast
and free-form
jazz and poetry.
Create a windy beat
to a jovial busker,
to a raging sea,
to a calm,
course sand,
to a wanderer who is
not all there.

Adapt to fire damage:
The faraway myrtles,
didgeridoos,
River Gum nickname
mean nothing here
in acres of

California eucalypts.

Alert weary visitors,
calm restless natives.
greet oblivious passersby—
Lemon-cool impression:
Welcome, welcome, welcome, welcome. . . .

First Taste of Ocean Salt

I. GASP

What is this ocean?
It is anything but calm
or peaceful.
It can drag you in,
drown you,
steal your breath.

Years before I
could answer
with "Pacific,"
I breathed in
that ocean
and tasted it.

II. THE UNDER-THE-WAVES SHOW

The meaning of vast
entered my vocabulary
long before the word.

I do not mean
the vast ocean or
its endless horizon.

It isn't the ocean
or the horizon
of that day I recall.

I was very likely two
or three when
we visited the beach.

Mom wanted for me
to experience the ocean,
so she dunked me in.

I kept my eyes open—
The Pacific's underbelly
isn't turquoise or warm.

Its gray, sandy whitewash
is complemented by water
so cold, blue, and rapid-static.

An endless time
of unbearable
white noise, sand, sea, and salt.

I went visiting
past lives who
walked into the water.

Escaping their lives
by reaching
for the horizon's end.

It took years
for me to identify
all of them.

Stinging eyes,
gagging from salt.
Why did she do it?

I'll never know
if it was just her
being frustrated.

I was a slow poke,
but I later learned
that she was suicidal.

All I wondered
at the time was,
is she killing me.

She said she just
wanted for me
to experience the ocean.

Nature is rough,
which may have been
the intended lesson.

It is simply complicated,
as is life, as is memory,
as is love.

The Anglers

Rogue waves hit the anglers on the rocks.
Fish heads, shrimp, and earthworms serve as bait.
Anchor chains clang against the boat docks.
A ghost line weighed down by a milk crate.

It is bad luck catching white sea bass.
A fish spews its offspring clutch in shock:
Swimming fish to sea kelp and sea grass.
Fish heads scare the folks on the boardwalk.

They still fish against furious wind.
Securing every rod, reel, and hook,
they see to a propped pole's perfect bend.
"Stingers, throw-aways," but that pole shook.

All that action came from the ghost line,
cast in honor of a man long dead.
By the crate is a bottle of wine,
an offering made to "angler Ted."

"He's caught some halibut, yellow tail,
barracuda, mackerel, and shoes."
On the harmonica he could wail.
His song was "The Black-Eyed Susan Blues."

"He said his playing brought him good luck.
Of course, he had to take that elsewhere.
His voice went to Venice for a buck,
but he'd spend it on his return bus fare."

Twilight comes and the anglers must go.
"Goodnight my dear friend," in slow, soft speech.
Old men at the sea, today it is no,
but dream of your youth, young lions at the beach.

Mars Pacifico

Heeding to the great explorer's advice
on a 1521 visit with Magellan,
Mars Pacifico was happy with the name change.
Even though the explorer was wrong—
Water on the red planet was just an illusion,
Mars Pacifico drew calm from the ocean
and a rare, warlike calling from the Red Planet:
Both useful for conquering
imaginary windmills, Portuguese pirate ships,
and searching for *Victoria* (now Vicky)
in a brothers-and-sisters-from-other-planets spirit.

Mars Pacifico retold the stories of Magellan
and how he was right that the Pacific was peaceful
when the explorer first encountered it
in the strait between Chile and Argentina
(just near the bottom of the world):
The waves in the Atlantic were seven meters high
while in the west, they were about one meter.

At the Thrifty Drugstore downtown,
Mars Pacifico put in his four hours in a security uniform,
Hoping that when *Victoria* wandered in,
she'd find him stopping a shoplifter
or joking with young children.
(He had seen more potential in her
than anyone else she knew.)
He would buy her
a triple-scoop ice cream cone,
knowing that she'd be hungry
but happy enough to be with her hero.

Those willing to hear Mars Pacifico,
as he danced and waved about,
were all convinced
by his clarity, conviction, charm, and wit.
But, spending the time as he wished, he moved
on to another person, another mission,
pursuing *Victoria* (now Tory), wherever she may be.

Mars Pacifico knew how to tell a story
and then to dash off quickly,
learning from Magellan,
during his final turn in the Philippines,
that meddling in people's lives
could get you killed.

Sand Crabs

Dig a hole,
and they'll come
to greet you.

In water
that fills in
their brief space.

Their bright white
bodies swim—
no rhythm.

These small crabs
observe no
strict canons.

Hello and
Goodbye in
an instant.

The Sand Dune Witch

A sand dune witch lives alone, far away.
We'll visit her home by the end of day.
It's covered by the Black-Eyed Susan vine.
She'll offer us in for a bottle of wine.

Chorus:
Tra-la dee-da fiddle o' rue,
tra-la dee-da fiddle o' rue,
tra-la dee-da fiddle o' rue:
Fiddle o' rue, we'll have some fun.

Hiking that dune with our faces to the wind,
The sand in our eyes that witch did send!
And there we failed to sense her evil curse,
My friend, I fear our story gets worse.

Chorus:
Tra-la dee-da fiddle o'rue,
tra-la dee-da fiddle o'rue,
tra-la dee-da fiddle o'rue:
Fiddle o'rue, the tale we've spun.

That sand dune witch had opened her door.
A delighted grin frightened us to our core.
And under the spells that she knew by heart,
we were made to dance to the billy goat's fart.

Chorus:
Tra-la dee-da fiddle o'rue,
tra-la dee-da fiddle o'rue,
tra-la dee-da fiddle o-rue:
Fiddle o'rue, she had some fun.

With a smack on our heads and a hostile stare,
a black cat scratched us while in mid-air.
This greeting was our welcome to Hell.
Did you hear the sound of the death toll bell?

Chorus:
Tra-la dee-da fiddle o'rue,
tra-la dee-da fiddle o'rue,
tra-la dee-da fiddle o'rue:
Fiddle o'rue, dong-dong-ding-dong.

"Damn you, who've come to see an old witch.
You'll find out soon I'm a crafty bitch.
You'll be mine now; you'll suffer from pox.
But I'll keep you warm in this lovely box."

Chorus:
Tra-la dee-da fiddle o'rue,
tra-la dee-da fiddle o'rue,
tra-la dee-da fiddle o'rue:
Fiddle o'rue, our own coffin.

Waving her wand, she conjured the moon.
My friend gave a groan, he began to swoon.
This story's moral is don't mess with the old:
They'll freeze your tears as your heart grows cold.

Chorus:
Tra-la dee-da fiddle o'rue,
tra-la dee-da fiddle o'rue,
tra-la dee-da fiddle o'rue:
Fiddle o'rue, the witch had won.

Despite our fate, we made a mad rush,
past her door, past the beach salt brush.
Down the dune, and out to the sea,
to outrun a witch and to get ourselves free.

Chorus:
Tra-la dee-da fiddle o'rue,
tra-la dee-da fiddle o'rue,
tra-la dee-da fiddle o'rue:
Fiddle o'rue, we're on the run.

But as we passed the purple ice plants,
she captured me by the seat of my pants.
She gazed at me as she held me high,
"You foolish child," she gasped with a sigh.

Chorus:
Tra-la dee-da fiddle o' rue,
tra-la dee da fiddle o' rue,
tra-la dee-da fiddle o' rue:
Fiddle o' rue, our souls are done.

I shook her grip and we ran to the beach.
The waves became within our reach.
But our minds departed when we went to wade.
Here is the part when my song must fade:

Chorus:
Tra-la dee-da fiddle o'rue,
tra-la dee-da fiddle o'rue,
tra-la dee-da fiddle o'rue:
Fiddle o'rue, we'll miss the sun.

Four Winds

Run to catch the pickup.
It comes at five after two.
The fate is worse than death
if you miss it.

Silver spoon smell—
Ionized air and trouble—
That dreaded run,
upset by synesthesia.

A spaced-out wait
in mudslide rain.
"Stupid. Hey, stupid."
That's my ride.

Escapes the mind,
seeing past beach houses
with raindrops on lenses. . . .
Shoulder punches.

Beats windshield wipers
timed to radio songs.
Random giggles past
Birds of paradise.

Brentwood blahs,
Westwood woes. . . .
Eucalyptus pod thuds
the faculty brats.

Time gaps with
contexts lost—
Angry adults disrupt
my world.

"Oh, just get out."
An easy option.
To there we run—
Welcome figs, eucalyptus.

Uncoordinated games
on sand and concrete;
Hurried swing songs
fill the air.

Ongoing fibs about
lavish past lives,
superpowers, traveling,
and drowning.

Chatter-babble of
wrong facts and ideas
taught by adults,
spread vicious rumors.

Daydreams bring bliss:
Unite dumb space-outs,
magician fibbers,
whimsical songwriters.

Four Winds supervise
past lives running counterclockwise
on sand-scabbed shins
and snack tickets.

Marco's Sea Colony

A marine biology student at UCLA,
Marco worked part-time as a counselor
for Four-Winds Day Camp.

Frizzy-haired, wiry
in his early twenties,
Marco was not too old
for expeditions.

From school to school,
he drove a van,
picking up kids on his route.
Summer was his favorite time of the year.

One year, he was assigned to my group.
Most of us were about seven or eight.
We called it "latchkey kid day camp,"
though our workaholic parents
wished we'd avoid such fate.

One day, Allen and I
were the only kids
on his early route.

Marco used the time to take
us to the Santa Monica Pier
to enjoy our very first boiled crab.

"They boil it in Pacific Ocean juice."
But he was kind and offered us both
the best meat on the crab.

"OK. Anatomy time!"
He flipped the crab over,
identifying everything
he could see
without hesitation.

"Now it's your turn."
Allen was the first
to break into laughter,
tell him "ew,"
but we were curious.

Allen and I
were the first kids
to get into rollicking rounds
of "Marco—Polo."

We theorized that
in his previous life,
he was the explorer,
driven by his knowledge
of the sea,
and a desire for
confronting creatures.

Our adventures carried on
to many days on the beach.
"Kids should play outside."
But Allen, me, and Paul Montgomery?
We were blondes and red heads.
Our mothers made us stink
of heavy sunscreen.

During that summer,
I had to play with boys
because of my plain bathing suit:
All the girls had pointed out
that it was a boys' suit;
therefore I must be a boy.

It was fine because
that meant more time
with Allen, Paul Montgomery,
and our resident
marine biologist.

Marco once told me,
"You're really cool.
You don't run away
from the gross things."

One day, Marco swam
about a half mile
to a massive bed of kelp
on Santa Monica Beach.

Allen, Paul, and I
took to our usual
dig to China—
as close to the pier
as possible.
We despised the sun.

"Come over here, you three!"
Marco returned.
He dragged out of his backpack,
Styrofoam cups,
and an empty plastic jug.

"Oh, cool! Cups!" Allen said.
"No, this," Marco pointed
to a giant, spongy brain-like sea colony
and explained what it was.

"We aren't going to keep it,
but it will be yours for the day."
We had no idea
what he was getting at,
but it sounded more interesting
than getting to China.

"Everyone gets a pet,"
he shouted,
but the other kids
naturally ignored him.

But some went over
to see what he was doing.
They walked away,
thinking that their pet for the day
would be a kelp floater
or something that could bite.

"My friends,
a tide pool has nothing
compared to the weirdness
you are about to experience.
Welcome to the hood.
The tide pool is like a suburban village
to where the real culture is at."

He poured sea water
into all the cups
and gently doled out
our pets for the day.
"They will go back to the colony,
which will be returned before we go."

The best pets were
brittle stars,
segmented sea worms,
purple anemones,
and small sea cucumbers.

For a day,
really no more than an hour,
my charge
was a nameless brittle star,
who I imagined
missed its home.

Though fascinated,
I brought it back
to the colony.

"It wants to go back."
The graffiti isn't as good
inside a Styrofoam cup."

He smiled,
thanking me
for returning the cup,
no questions asked.

Marco kept to his promise
and swam the entire colony
back to the kelp bed.

Turquoise ocean waves
formed in high peaks,
revealing kelp—
someone released the Kraken.
Maybe so.

But it was grateful
for the safe return of its colony,
and it spared our explorer Marco,
so he could make discoveries
on another day.

Dig to China

1 2 3 4—And
why do you think to
dig deep below? Through
wet, heavy sand in
waves to and fro. De-
spite your good sense, you
dig down to China. De-
spite your good sense, you're
never a quitter. A
crab leads the way. You
want to dig further. The
older kids laugh, but
you'll show them that
they're wrong. There's
more than just sand when
digging on and on. There's
more than the pit that
fills up with water. There's
more than the tar mats that
stick to our cold feet. And
break . . . .

Pirate Ships

I sleep
through windy-road driving
and I wake
on sandy-mixed ocean.
Fog creeps
to drowsy-mind music
and fog makes
my blurry-eyed visions.
Oil rigs,
like flying-free Dutchmen,
Oil rigs
are touching their delft.
Suspend
all adult-like thinking.
Suspend
our going to school.
My friend,
our pirate-foes see us.
My friend,
I don't think they care.
I dream
in sleepy-beach cities.
I wake
to pirate ships there.

Undertow Villanelle

How peaceful it is to be dragged by sea:
A landscape crafted by this undertow.
Soft roar, these ocean waves have set me free.

Some struggle back to land and try to flee,
but death is calm—relax—for I should know
how peaceful it is to be dragged by sea.

The view of strange creatures will make some plea,
but fear is not for friends we see below.
Soft roar, these ocean waves have set me free.

My gaze, so full of salt and sand, shall be
the last I see—I let the ocean flow.
How peaceful it is to be dragged by sea.

Coast down the shelf, and letting go is key.
I harmonize with drowning water, so
soft roar, these ocean waves have set me free.

And now, the evening star has called for me.
Go eastward, waves: I drift from westward ho.
How peaceful it is to be dragged by sea.
Soft roar, these ocean waves have set me free.

Paisley Picnic Blanket

A blue and green paisley picnic blanket,
reversible, so choose which color you favor.

It was bought some time before or after I was born
at a store that accepted green stamps.

It was made of soft but durable cotton and was finished
with inch-long twisted fringing I unraveled when I was little.

That ancient blanket visited the beach or parks,
laid out as a temporary home no matter the occasion.

It washed like a dream, having never stained,
having always kept in good shape.

In the 1980s, it covered old sofas and chairs,
and in the 1990s it was used to move furniture.

It reminds me of ice cream socials, pizza parties,
and explanations to friends that we weren't poor,
just hippie-chic.

Venice Beach, Ocean Front Walk, ca 1978

Venice Beach, up the Ocean Front Walk,
march our curious, little cold-cream feet,
glancing at abandoned apartments
and blown-out sliding windows,
among a tarred-sandy landscape
of orange-dappled sunsets and oil-black palms,
where wet-sheet, condemned cottages,
Marilyn Monroe's sweet grandmother,
and little, precocious Robert Blake
with his punch-colorful language,
were no more,
Tropicana roses set their roots deep,
blooming bright their buds between
chain link fences and cracked aqua tiles.

Jacaranda

An embroidered landscape
of blue-lilac French knot flowers over
gray-red straight- and seed-stitched bark.

Jacaranda trees are a sign of spring,
even in upwardly mobile L.A.,
where so few enjoy embroidery.

During the weeks after my birth,
the Santa Monica streets were
lined with jacarandas.

Streets with state names
like Montana and Arizona
were no exception.

Clouds were supposed to be
like chain-stitched swirls of
periwinkle, azure, silver, and white.

Van Gogh must have spent
an entire morning with needle and linen
to make that sky.

And Egon Schiele helped him
make the splendid arches that
became part of my first ride home.

These would be my birth flowers:
Compliments to pearl and
the purple-pink Alexandrite.

Tapestries hope to have textures
that bring to mind the smell
of sweet flowers in the fog.

As musical as I have always been,
I have never heard a jacaranda tree
whistle a tango or call my name.

This imaginary heirloom
exists only in my mind
on my Birthday.

The Camera Obscura on Ocean, Santa Monica

Let's deposit IDs for a set of keys and up the steep stairs we'll go.
From a darkroom hole to a white table, shows a picture from a tiny light's
glow.
Pan the lens about, from the North to the South, just to see who resides below.
An upside-down view will appear to you, a beach world inside a vivid halo.

To delight sightseers, there's a lens that steers that makes past and present flow.
The Palisades cliffs with their long-ago riffs can be seen through this special
window.
On the Sunset Incline, built in 1899, the obscura keeps up with SaMo's tempo.
Bringing lives we adore to an ever changing fore, a bright sunny beachside
tableau.

From a full-circle view, see snow on a mountain, snow on a mountain, snow. . .
.
Lined with eucalyptus trees, Birds of Paradise please, down by the Pacific O.

Let's enjoy a free peak at some famous freaks in a house on Rolls Royce Row:
Louis B. Mayer's then Peter Lawford's grand view of the Westward ho.
While the actor greets, his brother-in-law meets his good friend Marilyn
Monroe.
Camped out in ocean air, the Secret Service there, shadowing them to and fro.

See a romance brew, and a Rat-Pack feud, the Gold Coast House gives us a
show:
Trysts with RFK at his "hideaway" and tangos with the Mafioso.
Those Blonde high heels and a blue-blood's squeals can preen a young man's
ego.
Exposed in the sun were their rowdy days of fun, bathing poolside on a pillow.

From a full-circle view, see snow on a mountain, snow on a mountain, snow. . .
.
Lined with eucalyptus trees, you can catch a sea breeze, down by the Pacific O.

Let's forward our flight to a flare-jeans site and a vision of an antihero.
As the great lens steers, that same house appears, now a *Pussy Cats* rented
chateau:
Lennon spends his lost weekends with friends, Nilsson, Moon, and Ringo,

turning Jack's old study into a room for his buddy, completing his dream studio.

Photo shots by May Pang, *Revolver* art by Voormann, kitty tunes by a young playfellow.

Floating voices of joy. Were they from a sex toy? Yodels prompt the foghorns' sore bellow.

Shines a full, ripe moon, the ambitious seagulls swoon as they fight for a strewn stiletto

From his wild exile to the Catalina Isle, Nilsson belts his weary, rock falsetto.

From a full-circle view, see snow on a mountain, snow on a mountain, snow. . .

Lined with eucalyptus trees, the panoramas tease, down by the Pacific O.

Mother of Pearl

Iridescent,
not fully understood:
Simple nacre
on a seashell,
grown platelet
by platelet.

Glisten strangely,
light against
rainbow sparks
while emitting
melodic dharma.

Knowledge
well earned
connects nature
to music,
to finger touches,
covering keys
on a saxophone.

My Diebenkorn World

I. "SEAWALL," 1957

In Berkeley
during Oxfords time,
a captured seawall: Concrete
reflecting wave energy—
the Pacific Ocean can keep it.

In flat fields
of sand and ocean
color, evoking stained glass—
Matisse opaqueness,
corrections exposed.

A bird flies above
in finger-smeared
multidirectional fragments
of sky and below—
Surprise! Bright yellow.

A play on horizons, the seawall
divides beach
and kelly-olive green grass,
blown and flattened
by capricious winds.

Such conservation
in the painting: A coastal defense
from momentarily low
abrasive waves, translated
to shapes and lines.

Up close,
the huge seawall lends
angled perspective, earlier
color choices, figures, mirages,
thinly whitewashed.

Photos play unexpected
see-walls. Here
a viewer's block,
smoothes Kandinsky lines, fades
impressions of Other apparitions.

On that edge against grass and sea,
I may be walking with others, bathed
in smooth, muted colors of Modern oil, warmed
by blue Romantic sun, looking on
to what is and what will be.

II. "HORIZON OCEAN VIEW," 1959

Berkeley—Limits no limits: Timeless
with an assigned year (1959)
in marine-layer light,
empty beach,
a shock of chartreuse
or light yellow hill,
telephone poles
or volleyball court? A cup—
coffee or tea? The artist's?
For a guest? Matisse,
Hopper,
all at once, indoor,
outdoor. Blue table,
turquoise wall;
A thick, rectangular ledge
suggests a window's
frame that offers
a near-perfect view, only
distorted by vertical lines.
Choose your horizon.
Always choose. Follow

gentle arcs of power or
net lines to a far-off beach,
a lifeguard's deserted lair
to beach and sand,
to cobalt color fields of ocean
and plain, powdery blue sky,
both stirred by the same
wind and hand. Movement
in short, brisk strokes. Choose,
choose your horizon. Choose
inside or outside—screen or fog—
Choose the cup
or to have eyes move outside.
Choose where the limitless
window ends
or begins, if at all. Distorted rocks,
a midway watercolor-like puddle.
Choose a focal point
or several perspectives.

1959 is the present moment.
The philosopher Berkeley
was correct: All we sense,
just is. This horizon ocean view
is a frame of mind.

III. "THE OCEAN PARK SERIES," 1967-88

It began with a humble thought
at Diebenkorn's studio,
gazing from his window view
to hills, to beach, to Ocean Park below.

In seductive blue-foggy light,
he made broad fields of sound to see.
As curator Bancroft said,
"He painted in riotous calm."

During protests at UCLA
against the war in Vietnam,
oil and charcoal came to canvas in riotous calm, in riotous calm.

Oil and charcoal came to canvas in riotous calm, in riotous calm.

The artist was 45,
but he found a way to to still inspire.
In California's years of fire,
he found a grand landscape to focus on.

And Bach's *Fortspinnung* played on,
pushing forward his early strokes.
But Mozart was more often there
joining, piecing, gluing developing shards from air.

During smoggy days in sunny L.A.,
orange haze touched by burning palm,
oil and charcoal came to canvas in riotous calm, riotous calm.
Oil and charcoal came to canvas in riotous calm, riotous calm.

Small excursions to Ocean Park,
a long series for a small landscape.
His lines much like Frank Lloyd Wright:
Open corners and angled planes with scaffolding.

He destroyed nos. 1 through 5.
Bodies emerged from his no. 6,
layered like a Fresnel lens,
in white, in gray, in pink, in brown, in blue rhythmics.

In the leap year of '68
when the world was such a crazy maelstrom,
oil and charcoal came to canvas in riotous calm, riotous calm.
Oil and charcoal came to canvas in riotous calm, riotous calm.

In its play with shapes, figures, and lines,
and evoking old aerial shots,
the series spoke in muted layers,
ghost colors—past choices that were all whitewashed.

The *pentimenti* tell a different tale,
of where the artist once had been,
overlapped in their show of peace
the strikes, the scrapes, the rage that's walled within.

While the President lied and resigned,
and a young girl burned by napalm,
oil and charcoal came to canvas in riotous calm, riotous calm.
Oil and charcoal came to canvas in riotous calm, riotous calm.

No. 19 with its bright white stripes
frames a gradient from lilac to blue,
but no. 80 is a muted yellow,
in stark contrast to the bright blue shapes of no. 92.

The triangles in no. 79
echo on the left hand side
against rectangles of blues, lavenders,
veils of aqua, and yellow, spanning canvas wide.

In the middle of a fuel crisis,
evening news about a firebomb,
oil and charcoal came to canvas in riotous calm, riotous calm.
Oil and charcoal came in riotous calm, riotous calm.

He ended with no. 145,
when the artist reached 65.
The late ones reveal folded planes:
Time folds back on itself in bird's eye view eye strains.

Through ghosts of early color decisions,
the fragments are never set in stone.
And the need for expressionist revisions
in a series that never leaves the artist alone.

While Reagan made the state a joke,
Cold War fears enter an old sitcom,
oil and charcoal came to canvas in riotous calm, riotous calm.
Oil and charcoal came in riotous calm, riotous calm.

Oil and charcoal came to canvas in riotous calm, riotous calm,
riotous calm, riotous calm. . . .

Grout Sealer

Leaks—
Sandy sealer,
sailors' fricatives.

Future forward:
flotsam found.

Survivors swimming,
sounding, signaling
frequenting sirens.

Hiss—
Sinking ships,
Further from seashore.

Spongy fuser:
signifies failure.

Structural sealant,
submerging smokestack,
formative stasis.

Drifts—
Sundries, seashells,
swirling formations.

Findings sifted:
Settled fragments.

Scavengers' findings,
favorable sales,
forever silence.

The Looff Hippodrome Carousel at Santa Monica Pier

On the old Newcomb Pier,
built in nine-teen six-teen,
stands the Looff Hippodrome,
housing ghosts on the scene.

A Victorian house,
touched by Byzantine style,
bringing East to the West,
topped with Spanish Moor tile.

Starting sightseers' walks,
the building helps mark
that *Daisy Clover* view,
famous buskers by dark.

Walk invisible dogs!
Go see gypsy hand tricks!
Know Santa Monica pier
concludes Route 66!

But dear to old children,
and younger ones, too,
is that Merry-Go-Round,
that bright musical zoo.

Inside the Hippodrome
by Charles Looff and son,
hand-crafted menagerie,
wood-carved, one by one.

From Denmark Looff came.
He took furniture pieces,
and whittled our friends
who danced on the beaches.

A Coney Island dream,
saddle blanket of blue,
the "Armored Looff Jumper"
was the star of the crew.

That fierce, little black horse
really knew how to fly,
then rocked babes to dreamland
to Brahms' Lullaby.

And 'round spun that platform,
a zoological blur,
at five cents per fare,
its engine would whir.

Then one day it sold.
It was 1939.
And the Parker Carousel
moved into that shrine.

And advances were made,
with its chariot cart.
It met popular demand.
It was state of the art.

It added some new songs,
including sea shanties,
and "Beautiful Dreamer"
for the lasses and dandies.

After eight solid years,
despite the ride's boon,
the Parker had sold.
It played its last tune.

Into the Hippodrome,
Number 62 came.
Built in 1922,
it had a large frame.

The Philadelphia Toboggan
Company Carousel
traveled from Ocean Park
and still worked very well.

Bedecked with round light bulbs,
sketched landscapes, looking glass,
it held twice as many;
It spun twice as fast!

And the gondoliers' song
accompanied the lyre—
A far cry from Looff days
on sweet Newcomb pier.

The corporate chains drool
at the Hippodrome's site.
They'll impose their sameness;
Their greed dampens light.

Gone Blue Streak Racer,
Aeroscape, and The Whip,
but the Hippodrome's there
to shelter your trip.

Came your turn, then my turn,
the celebrities we've missed.
Now ashes to ocean;
Now ghosts in the mist.

I feel them ride with me,
a horse that youth holds.
The past enjoys prancing
as the present unfolds.

Walk invisible dogs!
Go see gypsy hand tricks!
Know Santa Monica pier
concludes Route 66!

Still the calliope plays
with the ocean-cold wind.
All our carousel memories
reaching their end,
reaching their end,
reaching their. . . .

Driftwood

I am her,
and what
I've never
meant to be.
And you
wanted to know
where we went
after we were seen
and no compensation
made to us.

After the
Crane Wife
was seen
in the act
of creating
and left
her greed-curious
husband,
she flew
in the direction
of driftwood.

Away from Japan,
over North Pacific waves,
both tired
and angry
about greed-curious
companions,
who failed
to listen to her,
never themselves
learning from
their own mistakes.
And to leave her alone.

Fits and starts
of growing back
pulled-out feathers
after making
beautiful things.
So many
unnecessary
fights over
never being
what we're
meant to be.
And hearing
about what
we should be,
or add, or do
to our craft.

Whatever happens,
in wandering
loneliness
and learning,
these flights
over white waves
are far better
than greed-curious
lockups' forced
creative work.

So, she and I
wander, whether
in mind or spirit.
We wander,
since there is
no end
for the greed-curious
gone cruel
on land.

We wander
with driftwood
on open ocean,
for too many times
in fickle, well crafted,
grown-hostile-world
captivity,
we never
get asked to teach.

The Sunset Trail (The California Incline)

Wide-open view—
See sand cliffs,
then beaches,
chain link walking
overpasses
hovering over
the PCH,
Marion Davis's
perfect mansion.

Beyond
the big "W"—
Stark white,
Monstrous eyes—
the General Telephone
building,
hovering over
the PCH,
as if ready
to careen into
an already
expansive view.

A brief
birds eye view,
downhill—
World wide open—
The north
promises
car exhaust,
but Malibu
comes first.

Postcards recall
in less
modern times
(A Sunset Trail,
a Gold Coast
passageway),
and the view still
works for me:

On the
road again;
This is the end,
but not the end.

The West Coast Jazz Gypsies

Play "Springsville" for us
at free sets along the Pacific.

Drift in, gentle waves, to Black Hawk,
The Ash Grove, the Lighthouse Café.

Spend Sundays in San Francisco
with soft Guaraldi sambas.

Let bebop zip by as fast as it can,
passing us to catch its swift waft.

Soak up Mulligan like salt air at night
in dream-song with Baker.

Say goodbye to Art Tatum on the piano,
riding club gigs 'til his sunset.

Drive, *Miles Ahead,* at moonrise,
play "Springsville" for us.

Santa Monica Pier, El Niño, 1983

Storm swells in January,
Then El Niño came in March.
a crane meant to fix the lower deck
collided, thrashing, destroying
the outermost third
that led to Pacific endlessness.

The next day,
the mall was filled
with local newspapers
chronicling the irreparable mess.

Little button pins
sold by the dozens
in novelty shops read,
"I've lost a friend."

We went to Santa Monica,
visiting home
just for a day.
All I was able
to bring back
is this awkward,
discordant poem
and a messed-up torch song
running in my head:

"Why not take all of me?"
I hate being lonely without you.

Amethyst Sea Shells, Blue Mussels

Swept upon the sand,
they find their way to me
in fragmented forms,
wholesale abandoned,
entire mollusk homes.

The false trumpets play
a whirl of a song.
Through a whorl of a spiral
and aperture to apex,
the howling dervishes
make sudden sense,
shrieking like wind
from shell to ear,
to a budding
composer's mind.

But spindle-shaped
purple shells
contrast silent,
dark blue bivalves
with mysterious nacre
that still escapes
the knowledge
of a budding
scientist's mind.

Rush-Hour (Ad)Ventura

Smog-hazy beeps, seeing through the veil between Santa Barbara
and L.A., that's Blake Edwards, the Pink Panther, relaxing,
almost transfixed here in a jam on the PCH, staring, just jazz-hot staring
at the ocean, the savior of boredom. We find ourselves approaching
granny land, those tall street lights that scream here are a zillion or more
malls. Target, oh, thank God for Target, right next to
Chuck E. Cheese, stop-go-lowriders curse at the cycle, road raging
in a pea-green boat of car, a Plymouth, that is, to you. Bass bounce,
God Almighty, a little girl finds entertainment getting gum smack-stuck,
smack-in-the-middle of her dishwater blonde Dutch-boy bangs, she shakes
her little pink Shirley Temple sponge curlers left, then right, then left, and
whack! Right against the passenger's windshield, good going with that whiplash,
little bored girl, your "Good Ship Lollipop" ride to grandma's has you seeing
stars, funny bangs, and a fat lip, among countless dusty lemon groves, rolling
down flat curves and smelling burnt trailer garbage, bacon
anyone? Eva Gabor's Buick moves at five miles per hour towards
her off ramp, where her driver takes his cue, makes his signal, and a good time
will be had by all at the Pic 'n' Save.

Beware of Underwater Obstructions

Like the way
I hammer against
this bass,
some foundations
are meant
to cut through you,
down to the bone.

Like the way
I grate my bow against
these strings,
some foundations
are meant
to knock the air out of you,
drowning
every fire you built
above ground.

Like the way
I tug thick strings against
this neck,
some foundations
are meant
to pull you in,
to remind you
to watch yourself
on your next swim
'round these parts.

The Beach Garden

Very alive and well,
Leo Gardiner,
sitting peacefully in
lotus position,
gives his love a ring on
an imaginary telephone in
his posh Received Pronunciation, he
explains to Mme. Rothschild that
he is at his tiny beach garden
office on the Riviera—No,
the Santa Barbara Riviera—and
cohabiting with the Italian Stone Pines and
the dry Mediterranean chaparral. The King
of Dutch Indonesia is sipping
Turkish coffee
with one of the make believe Grimaldis, you know,
the one who jet sets just
to arrive in your living room. As
they wait for de Firmian's yacht—you know,
the one painted in Habsburg yellow—they explore
fountains of fuchsia and passion flowers
while nibbling on false
cranberries and kumquats.
Once everyone gets here,
Let the Gatsby parties begin:
The Hoi polloi are welcome
to remain uninvited so they
can watch them from
their juniper hedges.
Oh, the enviable lives
of Santa Barbara's mildly schizophrenic royalty!

Brown Pelicans at Hendry's Beach

At Hendry's Beach,
some cross-cut barbeque French fries
have become popular snacks
for some seagulls,
but the brown pelicans
aim for bits of fish bait.

They swoop in majestically,
as if everyone fishing should
stop and notice,
at least say,
"You have a lovely beak, my dear,
and what a magnificent wingspan."

But the ravenous seagulls
ignore them,
and those fishing
laugh at their
clumsy landings and
their huge pouches.
Young children,
who don't know better,
stomp at the big birds,
who stand their ground
and wonder why
with their big, brown eyes.

Dog walkers from Hope Ranch
were the worst offenders,
which made their houses ripe targets
for any bird who has
had enough
dealing with the nouveau riche.

The brown pelicans at Hendry's Beach
are characters looking for plays,
but seem to get just close enough
to be associated with poems:
"Why, hello there, Ogden Nash."
But that is not *that* brown pelican's name.

He'd much prefer
Dixon Lanier Merritt,
or if you knew him better
he'd be fine if you called
him "Belican the Pelican"
because you'd still be correct.

As a theatrical bird,
(if you sit quietly for long enough),
Belican will recite passages
from his favorite monologues;
He'll throw in some pantomime,
if you tip him well.

In a large sand pit,
other brown pelicans huddle
together and discuss their dreams
of appearing in Albee,
show stealing in Beckett,
or flying in David Lynch.

They are pleased that finally
an adoring fan has left them
some fish tacos.

Fight Against the Tide

Alas,
the tragedy of sand castles,
and sand mound fortresses,
washed out by waves!

Their tiny motes
were futile defense
against the current,
and the angry tide.

All great kingdoms
crumble to nothing,
some became temporary
tide pools for sand crabs.

These loyal serfs
dig down deep below
false foundations
ironically avoiding the surf.

The nobility
cannot be found.
They escaped or
were drowned.

That tide took out
a cultural mecca
with no thoughts
and no regrets.

What the world
will miss by this
indiscriminate,
natural disaster.

The strand is
now a clean slate.
My kingdom lasted
a moment longer
than my friend's.

I win.

Bamboo Bong

My bamboo bong deserves a song:
It's crafted with great care.
I sawed the wood that made it good;
It will survive some wear.

I like to take it to the beach,
or hit it in my den.
I know you shit-faced drunkards preach
and tell me it's a sin.

My bamboo bong is never wrong:
It pays your way to learn.
And those who weep can go to sleep,
and calm that toss and turn.

The "Maha Mantra," Then Danceaway

What a wild night
it was, we kids,
with rosy health food cheeks
without a plan ended
at a Hare Krishna chant—zills,
we mean zills and tambourines, chanting
of pure love or whatever the you-God
wants to make it to be. Burning bright
candles, flickering against Krishnas
and Ramas and perpetuated dharmas, all
in midair, some closed-eyed loveliness:

Hare Krishna, hare Krishna,
Krishna, Krishna, hare, hare.
Hare Rāma, hare Rāma,
Rāma, Rāma, hare, hare

Like collecting flotsam, we
never forget what we've picked up,
on which we focused through chant
and song with zills and tambourines,
inhaling and exhaling sea air and
pot resin. We kids would stunt
our growth once more inhaling, too,
the circulating vibes of chants, candles,
tambourines, and zills:

Rāma, Rāma, Rāma, Rāma

Orange, we looked at the energy in
everyone's eyes, seeing
who just is and isn't—Eye Gods laugh and drift.
Leaving lotus footprints, we dash
to our Danceaway, a little sock hop
with outdated '80s songs. And
blissed-out chanters, now ready
to dance the pure love of God (Krishna) in
a Universalist church with bare feet to
in a Golden Earring twilight zone,

The Dazz Band lets it whip, search
for a flute playing Vishnu, or Siddhārtha Gautama,
and the joy-smiles of other dancers
swinging on their paths.

Rāma at the Waves

A brief adventure on LSD:

Just a few hundred years after Varuna promised to keep
the oceans still for my passage,
I, Rāma (seventh avatar of Vishnu)
in perfect blue man form
have decided to walk past the waves,
offering to share dharma
with a 1980s Sunburst style commune (in utopian exile)
in Santa Barbara, where I walk from East Beach,
through Spanish-tiled downtown, beyond the bus depot
to West Valerio Street,
knocking down some wise slam poet. I
move forward to meet my friend Elbridge Bill Hathaway—
Portuguese linguist, American diplomat's son, Stanford alum,
lead scholar and manager of the hippie intelligentsia,
translator of the *Dervish Diary*. He
lives in the front house. I,
Rāma greet the grumpy guru,
who once conversed with Huxley and Rexroth
under bright red pepper trees, who also
owns a rat-infested book shelf of smelly books—
I want to read all of them.
Bill once got a nine-year old hooked
on Fitzgerald's translation of *The Rubáiyát of Omar Khayyám*
and Huxley's *Island*, Orwell's *Animal Farm*. He
is reclusive,
but loves the company of smart Titian red heads—
An independent bookstore owner, a single mother,
someone named Gertrude, who made knowing jokes
about Laplanders drinking elk piss. . . .
She was the real thing and had grown up there. I
know to offer Bill Portuguese sherry
to gain admittance. His neighbor,
a homeopath nicknamed "Medusa Head,"
had fled to New York after renting a place
he didn't own
to collect money to disappear. Chants of my name
waft through the air, punctuated by clanging zills. I,

through thick bamboo, where another homeopath lives
with his daughter. Isis greets me, knowing my destination. We
drill holes in bamboo, to make a flute for a friend
and tend to mushrooms hidden in a garage. I,
Rāma, come to share teachings here, passing the ocean,
in perfect form, fasting, drinking sherry,
hearing dharma, observing the g uru
in old man form, holding himself together,
not putting up with the world's mumble-jumble anymore,
read passages from Dass's *The Psychedelic Experience*,
meditate, focusing on the I-God, the You-God, we
drift in Padma's lotus footsteps through wind chimes
and unlocked doors, go outside to perform Tai-Chi,
facing the waves I have left, transferring ether to radiating sun,
looking for energy in the air that is
neither created nor destroyed
too easily.

Radha's Red Nash Rambler

I miss the bumpy rides in Radha's red Nash Rambler.
She'd turn "Cecilia" on full blast;
It just happened to be on the radio.
We loved this part of the journey.
Josh and I would lie down on the back seat
because she was driving down Chapala Street.

The car would fly from bump to dip,
And we would levitate briefly,
sometimes hitting the old car's roof,
and coming down laughing,
we'd bounce up again
from the seat's industrial strength springs.

Cecilia would break our hearts,
shaking our confidence,
pothole after pothole,
dip after bump,
rock after rock.
and she wasn't coming back.

We'd all laugh-sing,
and belt our giddy, hiccupping woahs
pretend Indians cupping hands to mouths.
We had known that the red Rambler
was good for ridiculously bumpy rides
that accommodated our young imagination.

We'd clap our hands
and drum on the sides of the car.
We were so small that one of us
too often landed on the floor of the car.
Josh and I would just lie down again,
prepared to take another bumpy flight.

"You're going to break the axle on that car,"
our skeptical folks would warn us,
half laughing at our story.
but in no way did that ever stop us
for we had a healthy dose of childhood wonder
and we were full of hippie optimism.

Knots

I'm a macramé genius,
an expert at tying knots,
from my school days learning to tie my shoes,
to my favorite pastime while my family argued.

I have admired knots on ships and piers,
my eyes and hands followed stitches and weaving,
I worked to reproduce them as miniatures,
to secure my brocade blazers.

As I became older,
I liked to use my hands
and I'd take crafts classes
just to make all kinds of knots.

In high school,
I would sell my knots
either at a swap meet or on boardwalks
where neo-hippies had to have them.

At the time,
I'd call them friendship bracelets,
and you'd believe me when I'd tell you
they'd bring you more friends
or at least some good karma.

What surfer, beachcomber, dreamer
would be without my colorful knots,
my designs,
my own little puzzles of wonder.

While not out making a living,
I tied many knots in school—
Impressive knots—
To my teachers' frustration and delight.

As sources of controlled creation
combined with safe repetition,
my knots both took me places
and strangled me.

My writing knots have had their share of critics:
"You should unpack your sentences,"
"We can't accept this triangulated perspective,"
"This thread needs woven in better."

Mastering the smallest form,
supporting great ideas,
my knots were more admirable
as small, self-contained projects.

So, I turned away from writing,
to go back to making knots for sale,
but my hands are not as strong,
and my fine-motor coordination
not nearly as brilliant.

Others have now learned
to sell their knots on the beach,
what they lack in innovation,
they make up for access of materials:
The shells I used as beads
are no longer innovative details.

As much as I love making knots,
I don't teach others to make them,
for they can take you to places
yet they can also strangle you.

I'm learning to unravel knots,
or at least to finish them off
before I run out of time,
following their stitch and their weave—
Reversing—
An obsessive desire of controlled creation.

But you'd believe me
as I tell you how beautiful they were,
for I'm a macramé genius,
an expert at tying knots.

The Fog Monster

Push off the sun.
Limit visibility.
Touch eyes,
touch sandy cliffs,
touch park gazebos,
touch automobiles.
Slow down
everything
to a sleepy, gray crawl.

May wise
children utter,
"Yay, darkness"
to praise you,
and ingenious
weathermen
honor you with
sea foam green t-shirts.

Cool June
like every
January elsewhere.
Drift timelessly
my lonely way,
so that I
can smile at you,
loving that
sometimes
in this world
the monsters win.

Walk on Water

As a young child,
Anne always envisioned
going on great adventures.

Vivid dreams would come
of driving a car—
No destination required.

To go to sleep at night,
to herself she told a story
about rowing a boat to nowhere.

Voices were not always simply voices,
but sometimes they told her
what to do and how far she could go.

As a teen, Anne loved painting walls,
sharing her visions of God,
using bright shades of red.

On her better days,
Anne was everyone's
most fun college friend.

Out of the blue,
a postcard came:
Anne made it to Spain.

We'd be glad for her,
for she had the nerve
to experience whatever she wanted.

The quietest student,
then a fiery artist
on a stuffed shirt's radar.

Anne knew a secret:
If she disappeared,
she could get to nowhere.

Mental health volunteers
came over to her house
to see how she was doing.

She was their favorite medium,
but on her final journey,
she stayed away from home.

Across the street, we once spotted her
with a shrouded Jesus group
(that's what everyone called them).

One day in the local thrift store,
we overheard her mother
telling others how she left.

On a walk to East Beach—
Anne drifting, splashing, and talking
to an imaginary someone.

Voices were not always simply voices,
and the ones who told her how far she could go
did not find a boundary that day.

Walking deeper into the ocean,
walking on water in her mind,
Anne took a visit to nowhere.

Gypsy Boots Was Here

Gypsy Boots was here.
with tunes in his head,
he performed Russian dances
his mother had taught him.

A fitness pioneer,
an actor, a writer,
he led summer solstice
with bells on.

He lived as a tribesman,
loved hiking and yoga.
He slept in oak trees;
He bathed in hot springs.

Blessing the ocean,
and hugging the sunshine,
he led summer solstice
with bells on.

His friend eden ahbez,
had penned a song on him,
that made Nat King Cole,
a popular hit.

That fine "Nature Boy" who
grape-vined down State Street,
he led summer solstice
with bells on.

He married a dancer,
a young Lois Bloemker,
and started his Health Hut,
all decked with bamboo.

Yet ever a figure
of our counterculture,
he led summer solstice
with bells on.

Steve Allen had loved him.
He appeared on his talk show
twenty-five times,
and swinging off vines.

That smoothie creator,
organic juice maker,
he led summer solstice
with bells on.

In *Mondo Hollywood*,
a classic cult movie,
Bootzin played himself
in a narrating role.

A fireball of energy,
and all from clean living,
he led summer solstice
with bells on.

Gypsy Boots was here.
and it's no surprise
that his folks
were well versed in Ragtime.

With honed syncopation,
a whoop, and a holler,
he led summer solstice
with bells on.

The Sex Wax Punks

Liberty spikes—Genuine liberty spikes!
For about 15 minutes the home of the
Egg McMuffin became the
Sex Wax punk mecca of the universe.

In studded leather jackets,
dog collars, multiple piercings,
eyeliner, lipstick, skinny stirrup pants, and tatts,
they were all done up, but not feeling special.

They sported their Mohawks;
some looked like Foghorn Leghorn
with music in their heads
and a beach to go visit.

I was jealous, but I was just nine
when I first discovered
Santa Barbara's Sex Wax punks,
and too uncool to approach them.

Before they'd head down to East Beach,
one of them needed to pick up
some stationary from the Paper Star,
a quaint card shop at the front of a mall.

Sex Wax offered the convenience
for these kids to be punks
just for the weekend and
"Normal" school kids the rest of the time.

Do It Yourself,
except for food,
except for the stationary,
but they otherwise looked the part.

They did their own hair.
My mom said I could not get
my own jar even though
my allowance covered it.

She still liked watching them, too.
I wanted to grow up to be one,
not realizing I was closer to their ages
than my mom dared to tell me.

"And because I said, 'no,'
doesn't mean that you get to
shoplift a jar, do you hear me?"
She had me at my go-around.

Butterfly Beach

Our muses have the same address:
As artists, we're left with this diminishing sea strand.
Our wild ways reduced to tide pools
that don't really want us.

That didn't matter.
We'd walk there anyway,
ambitious dreams between our ears
and sand between our toes.

A long, faraway walk back and forth,
subtext allowed, but subtitles not included:
This walk is open for interpretation.
Never collect a muse that you cannot house and feed.

The Shark Purse

There's a shark purse on the beach here,
and its presence gives folks a fright:
Tourists depart while natives cheer here.
Mamma Shark is on the site.

That gray sand shark, she's a tiger
with needle-sharp teeth to eat small fish.
If you greet her, just don't fight her.
Body surfers aren't her dish.

Ever buoyant in the surf zone,
Mama Shark just likes to swim.
She's not known for biting humans,
or wave waders, on a whim.

You can't guess why, she makes her swim here,
but you'll find out at the moon.
In the sea waves, she likes hunting
to a cool or hot jazz tune.

By the Biltmore, Coral Casino,
play the duo called Hank and Wayne.
On the trumpet, with a straight mute,
Joey D. blew *Sketches of Spain.*

Just at ten sharp, they play jazz standards
poised to boost a dull night life:
Monk's "'Round Midnight," Hoagy's "Stardust,"
not to mention "Mack the Knife."

Butterfly Beach loves its Haifisch,
with her shark purse that glitters bright,
and the Biltmore will be boppin'
when Mamma Shark comes back tonight.

Olive Mill Bistro, Montecito

Dixieland mood adjustment, touched
by sprays of freckled Peruvian lilies, flown in
from Bogota, Santiago, and Lima, sisterly
are the bartenders, happiness transmitted
and smile-delivered by Paul and Max, who
invested and continued this mecca
for adults preferring Al Hirt over much
sillier venues for their nightlife pleasures, bringing
New Orleans lagniappe to paradise every Saturday
or Sunday.

Don't rest in peace. Keep the upbeat tempo going:
Memories still need to waft sweetly into the night.

Morning Stroll

Early one morning,
my mother woke me up
to take a stroll
at La Cumbre Plaza,
an outdoor mall,
in Santa Barbara.

As a teenager,
who took more offense
to waking up early in the morning
than the offer of a mall jaunt,
I could not understand
why we needed to go there.

Mom had been out
most of the night,
going between
Dixieland jazz at the Bistro
and a party in the green room
at the Lobero Theatre.

Going out was part of
her depression therapy,
allowing her to try on
her best Marilyn Monroe,
Jane Russell,
or Hard-Hearted Hannah.

"Give the people
what they want to hear,"
the psychiatrist said,
"And if it takes
another personality,
that's OK."

Enjoying loneliness
since an early age,
I played record albums
until midnight,
taking dictation on
Johnny Cash songs.

In that time
I learned excerpts of Bizet,
belted with Tom Jones,
tap danced to musicals,
hid from Mussorgsky,
and zoned out to *Music for Zen Meditation.*

It was too early to wake up
for a morning stroll,
and too early
to go to the mall
to window shop
or to people watch.

Yet there we were,
walking from Sears,
passing by the Laurel Burch store,
Williams-Sonoma—
All still closed
at this ungodly early hour.

But we were not alone.

In front of us,
walked a well dressed,
tall, slender, aristocratic man—
Staggering a bit
and clearly shaking off
a hangover.

He stopped in front of
Brooks Brothers,
perhaps looking
at silk ties,
three-piece suits,
or fine, dapper suspenders.

"That man
is the great
Shakespearean actor,
John Carradine,
and you likely
do not know him."

"He's Kung Fu's dad,
and I can see
the resemblance,
but I don't know him
from anything else
or why we're watching him."

"You don't know him,
but you know of Mel from
the television show *Alice*
with Vic Tayback,
who I just found out
is a good friend of Carradine's."

"Last night,
I saw the two of them
in the Lobero green room,
and they were having
so much fun that they sung
'Over the Rainbow' at least five times."

Many years afterward,
I learned of Carradine's work;
Not just as a Shakespearean actor,
but more as a reader
of jazz poetry
on now-obscure spoken word records.

The charm of him
partying with Tayback,
singing "Somewhere Over the Rainbow,"
matches the wonderful irony
of now knowing Rexroth's poem,
"Thou Shalt Not Kill."

The final angry lines,
directed at the listener,
who killed
Dylan Thomas
with one's
Brooks Brothers suit.

I do not believe
that Carradine
was so self-aware
of that very moment
when he took
his morning stroll.

Featured Artists at the Miramar

Upon this sea view
near Carpinteria, more fondly known as "Carp,"
creative luminaries offered workshops,
intersecting their writerly lives
with our emerging aspiring ones.

For twenty dollars per workshop,
Charles Schultz, Ray Bradbury,
Steve Allen, and Jonathan Winters,
would quietly converse
on their crafts.

Schultz and Bradbury loved
the spirit, the drive to draw or write;
Allen would converse while on piano;
Winters wrote about his characters,
getting them just right.

For a while, teachers loved
Finding their way to the Miramar.
Curiosity led to lessons everywhere there,
all while Al Reese and Robin Frost
played ragtime in the neighboring lounge.

An out-of-place kid could get a first-class education
on writing, art, and music.
Sound recording engineers,
who guarded their secrets,
would open up and willingly share their knowledge.

Upon this sea view
near Carpinteria, more fondly known as "Carp,"
teachers came and went,
but I recall these moments
when the Miramar was much more than a hotel.

Swimming to the Channel Islands

Twenty-two miles
seen as just one mile
within the mist
of a low fog trick
and a deceptive tidal calm.

This sunny afternoon,
the buoys and pelicans
will have ice-cold visitors waiting,
and the California Coast Guard,
will offer a no-frills cruise home
to the duped ocean swimmers.

Red Tide

The beaches are haunted
by *Karenia brevis*,
who enjoys her own spring
every time *El Niño* comes around.
She stinks to high heaven:
Imagine rotten fish for three full days.
And the sea is not blue,
or green with blue waves,
or blue with gray waves,
or gray with white waves.
None of them is strange,
with dead kelp like brown lace
and displaced mussel beards.
People should stay away
from her toxic bloom and maroon roses.
A drunk sailor can have her.
He should take her out West,
show her his boots,
and tell her tales about capturing tigers
under a delightful, red sky.

Ralph!

Ralph! Ralph!
The purple heron
wants to arrange a
meeting with you.
Let's make it
tonight during
your rendezvous.

He looks into
your big brown eyes
as you stare out of your
companion's panoramic view window
on the second floor
of his bungalow.

He will bring his friends
to come sit on a
tall palm tree,
watching you drink.
Your wine serves
as foreplay
to his orgy.

Your companion
sure loves those
Lotte Lehmann Lieder recordings.
Ralph would also like
to meet a bird
named Sieglinde,
to take
on slow,
majestic flights.

"Is it a good year?"
Ralph addresses you
with his purple heron squawk.
The zinfandel is what it is.
He has no inhibitions,
though a casual meeting
nevertheless requires
an appointment.

He wants to let you know
that this year
in Goleta,
by the airport,
the fish have been especially good,
and the natives offer Ralph
and his friends more
because they think they are storks
and storks are good luck.

Ralph loves this sophisticated life,
standing on palm fronds,
people watching,
and taking a part in your
little nightcap.
He laughs at your
friend, the drunk Irish judge
(listening to his phonographs),
who wants you
to be his mistress.

After all,
the old man's plumage isn't nearly
as outstanding as his.

New Zealand Spinach against the Sea Spray

Here is a place
to rest your bike
and lie among
soft ground cover
as the tide comes in.

Taste salt spray,
yellow mustard,
and sea rocket
kin to radishes.

Yellow-green,
mealy-bland,
the sea spinach
wins the contest.

The hardest seeds
always need nicked
to make their way
to next year.

Vistas of Isla

I. HIGH TIDE

Parking our bikes on New Zealand Spinach,
Josh and I head downstairs to the Isla Vista beachfront.

Wading barefoot in side-splashing waves
against a bluff, our tiny strand diminishes and
quickly we find ourselves in deep water.

There will be no walking to the Channel Islands today.
Like that would ever happen, but why not imagine it?

Instead, our fortunate hands find the stair rails.
As five-minute sea monsters (masters of the doggy paddle),
Josh and I pull ourselves out of the high tide.

II. ABALONE TREASURE

Up the tower,
ascending six
maybe seven
stories from
a spiral staircase of
an apartment complex
amusingly called
"The Penthouse"
(owned by
a crazy-angry
Hungarian slumlord),
Josh and I wanted
an aerial view of I.V.,
his neighbors' chickens,
and his father's
hippie-bong
college den.

Rock-covered roof,
decorated with drying
abalone shells—

A diver's lucky treasure.
They'd sell
at the swap meet,
and there
were so many.
This was better
than swiping
the neighbor's
rusty-nailed wood
for fort making.

That Christmas,
everyone we knew
received an ashtray.
We were good kids.

III. DUMPSTER DIVING

I resent. I don't want to be seen.
I resent. I'd be humiliated if someone knew us.
I resent. I can't stand the smell.
I resent. My mother would dig through it with a broken golf club.
I resent. I had to stand around for hours while she did it.
I resent. Josh got lice from wearing an unwashed hat.
I resent. I didn't want to be found for lice at school.
I resent. The on-the-bluff apartments and frat houses were gorgeous at $3000
          per month.
I resent. There were always amazing views of the beachside, bluff, and campus.
I resent. The weather always cooperated when my mother planned our
          dumpster diving.
I resent. The place had a population density that was greater than Calcutta.
I resent. Isla Vista was full of middle-of-the street sofa skeletons after nightly
          bonfires.
I resent. We had to compete with the Hmong residents for the good stuff.
I resent. On a dive, my mother once found a mink stole and a working stereo.
I resent. I found a script to a perverse production starring Sigourney Weaver.
I resent. I pretended to be a correspondent to a found postcard from Wales.
I resent. If you were from Cardiff and got puzzling letters, sorry I messed with
          your mind.
I resent. My mom could take on aliases from thrown away driver's licenses.
I resent. The end of the spring semester brought us bags of dirty, free crap.

I resent. I liked the free things after my mother washed them.
I resent. It was fun testing out things we wouldn't have bought on our own.
I resent. I liked the unopened containers of food left on the curb.
I resent. I was able to pay for tuition for four summers with ditched
          schoolbooks.
I resent. We sold the garbage back to students who wanted to recycle clothes.
I resent. I avoided summer work and began my own garbage tie-dying empire.
I resent. I had the best dorm room furniture when I went off to college.
I resent. The brats' parents who bought them new stuff to replace the stuff
          they threw out.
I resent. The fact was that we couldn't survive without dumpster diving.

IV. THE MAGIC LANTERN

Across the street
from the Autohaus,
the Magic Lantern
would show
evening matinees.
Josh and I
would go by bike
to bring his dad
his lunch.

When he wasn't busy
fixing BMWs,
soldering worn-out tools
to make new chess pieces,
or revamping an old DC-5
into a luxury trailer
fit with a running Jacuzzi
(which required a lot of pot),
Jason would create new signs
from the Magic Lantern's letters.

That night,
after the showing
of Bakshi's *Wizards*,
during a production
of *The Rocky Horror Picture Show*,
Jason and his friends
would drive into the Magic Lantern
on their motorcycles,
doing their best
Meatloaf impersonation.

This is just one reason
Josh loved his busy dad.

Sand Cricket Song

Riff, riff, cricket, riff—

<<pentatonic bass>>

Cricket, riff, riff—SHARP!
SHARP! SHARP! SHARP! Riff, riff.
Ssss. Sssssssss. Riff. Cricket.

<<cymbal and high hat>>

Sssss. Riff. Cricket. Riff.
SHARP. <<clavés click>> Riff.

<<pentatonic bass>>

Riff, riff, cricket, riff—
Ssss—riff, riff, riff. Sssss.
Cricket—riff , cricket.
Riff—cricket—riff—riff.

Sssss. Riff. Cricket—riff.
SHARP! Sharp <<clavés click>>.

<<cymbal and high hat>>

I flicker my sound
with friends on a hill.
You're never alone
when a cricket sings.

I dassssssh in five-four
timing, rubbing my
sandy legs to make
two and—three beat groups.

<<pentatonic bass>>

SSSSHARP! SSSSHARP! Cricket riff.

1-2, 1-2-3;
1-2, 1-2-3.

Four legs and this sand,
I march and I waltz.
You dance in your head
and sleep to my chirps.

We tend to invade,
but the solo here
soothes your loneliness,
and you feel alive.

A move. Riff. A strike.
A dance. Riff. A spark.
Matchbox, saccharin—
Lighter, fortunate.

In ether. Riff, riff.
you hear my dashed words.
Whisper, sardonic—
You link their meanings.

<<clavés click>> Riff. SHARP!

And now you get it:
"Strangers in the night,"
a source of standards,
a nightly torch song.

"Take Five," "Fascination,"
Martin Denny songs,
Davis, Ellington—
Riff—I, Cricket—Riff.
<<guiro scratch, cymbal>>

Max Roach had come up
with his ride cymbal—
Soft beats for solos
wafting in the air.

<<pentatonic bass>>

Bobby Darrin got
his famous phrasing,
eliding here, where
Coltrane found the West.

Cricket—riff—riff—dash,
Cricket—riff—riff—Ssss.
Four legs scratch this sand,
and "A Love Supreme."

<<music fades here.>>

Dolphins along the PCH

The dolphins swim, rolling,
rolling near the ocean shore,
touching that deep sandy floor,
leaping in the air to soar.

The dolphins swim, rolling,
rolling near the ocean shore,
racing past your wheels of four,
taking turns and keeping score.

The dolphins swim, rolling
rolling near the ocean shore,
stirring up the tidal bore
laughing at their fun encore.

The dolphins swim, rolling. . . .

Rincon

Come catch some waves,
wrestle with the "Queen of the Coast,"
climb a tree for red plantains across from the Cove,
sing your favorite songs from *Candy-O*,
forget that you're neither here nor there,
wave hello to a glimpse of Noah bobbing in the ocean,
sport a bleached blonde flat-top,
wear a surfer's wet suit everywhere you go
(including while on the bus),
turn your back to the drivers on the PCH,
meander alongside the Pacific coastline,
fit into a Beach Boys' song,
walk the nose and hang ten,
dance under a marine-layer blocked sun,
avoid the large, granite boulders during ocean swells,
and ride that long, beautiful wave into the sunset. . . .

Garbage Bonfires at the Emma Wood State Beach

The stench is somewhat reminiscent
of a campfire and toxic bacon.

Drivers hold their noses on the Pacific Coast Highway
as they must pass the bumper-to-bumper trailers.

They speed by a variety of trailer names and bumper stickers:
Winnebago, Volkswagen, Good Sam, AAA, Airstream. . . .

Not to mention, "The weather is lovely, wish you were here,"
and "My other car is a Rolls Royce."

Blake Edwards and Eva Gabor found themselves on many evenings
partaking this moment of Steinbeck's desperate-but-free California.

Yet the orange flames burn beautifully
against the purple sky, the silver clouds, and the turquoise ocean.

This is the cheap and clean way to live in California,
that is, if you own your own trailer and have no other cares in the world.

Here, you have the beach
and a way to get rid of your garbage.

You don't have to carry it around with you,
since there is a place for it every evening starting at 5 PM.

Mugu Rock at Point Mugu State Park

Always the passenger,
my one superpower
has been finding
signs that guide
us to a parallel universe.

To you, dear driver,
Mugu rock—Mugu:
the Chumash word for beach—
is that last giant rock
you see just before
plunging your car
into the ice cold Pacific Ocean.

You find it
on your maps,
today on your GPS.
Research offers,
whether you want it or not,
that it was created
when road workers
cut a path through
to make the Pacific Coast Highway.

Research offers,
whether you want or not,
the news stories
about stupid people,
who climb up
Mugu Rock's impossible incline,
maybe to fish,
maybe to cliff dive,
falling to their deaths
when a random wave
simply takes them out.

The outermost point
of the Santa Monica Mountains,
the point that juts out,
a jagged edge
on the California Coast,
recalls the old
Rancho Guadalasca Boundary.
That is, to drivers,
the "coastal headland promontory."

But your reality
ends here where mine
begins strangely:
At a certain angle,
Mugu rock
turns the horizon into
a flat surface
(two-dimensional),
perhaps a midair mirage,
perhaps my imagination
seen from
the passenger's side.

Swimmers may have tried
but failed to go through
the gateway physically.
Drivers who are dreamers
keep plunging their cars.
The one way
to get past Mugu Rock,
is with a wandering mind.

So, as you drive,
I ask that you stop
filling in the gaps
of silence
with conversation.
The other world
hates playing
second fiddle
to this one.

Kitesurfing at Zuma

Nameless faces,
hardworking hands,
greet you first:
Migrant workers
waiting
at the bus stop
on the edge
of a sunny
Malibu beach.

It is the same scene
with new characters,
but who recalls
the old ones?
Zuma Beach,
with its famous
clean water
and rip currents,
is always
equated
by the natives
with Steinbeck
and Guthrie
faces and hands.

They face north
at times to catch
a glimpse
of kite surfers
taking free rides
with fancy
leading edge
inflatable kites,
pulling on four lines,
gaining
much needed traction,
using their legs
and hands
for that great, long ride.

Flowing bow
and c-shaped kites
fill the sky
with bright
reds, greens,
yellows, blacks—
All reducing
nameless kite surfers
to faceless athletes
with tiny hands
pulling puppet strings.

Eyes gazing
on the soaring
freeriding kites
become entranced
by flight patterns
made by turning
feet and hands,
crashes in water,
and re-launched
kites of
anonymous friends.

An orange kite
flies away.
Still full of
salt air,
it rides
a wind current,
turns on
its own,
fighting wind gusts,
without hands,
yet facing
the sandy hills
across the
busy highway.

Isn't it wonderful
tracing
an orange kite
flying,
migrating,
drifting
above the clouds,
towards warm sun,
away from
faces and hands
with no names?

Saint Monica at Palisades Park

In dense fog,
by that eternal ocean,
settling down gently
below fig trees and
Japanese bank skyscrapers:
Ends the long stretch
of Wilshire
(past bakery, delicatessen,
shoe store, laundromat),
Saint Monica's
modern sculpture
welcomes her
wayward children
home.

Patron saint
of difficult marriages,
conversion of relatives,
victims of adultery
and verbal abuse,
and (most notably)
disappointing children,
her concrete image
faces the city;
her smooth back
to the sun.

In the thick midst
of the Great Depression,
she emerged from
the sculpturing hands of
Eugene Morahan.
In high art deco style,
she stands in hard sadness,
in perpetual prayer,
with hands crossing her heart—
a Public Works Art Project.

In reality, she frowns
and I just can't bear it.
She stands stark silently
in Palisades Park,
once upon a time
on a sweet heart-shaped bed
of dark green grass,
now rendered shapeless.
On some days,
the bright Pacific sun
turns her tall figure
from light gray
to white.

Maternal saint of
Great Depression existentialism:
Saint Monica is there
for unfaithful East coast runaways,
for unhappy children,
who find no solace
with Ferlinghetti's
lack of an angel,
not to mention
for those
just visiting again—
unsuccessful in
surviving her city's
common law ordinances
and gentrifications.

She welcomes us all,
even with her own
dreams unfulfilled,
disappointed.
And yet she continues
to hold onto hope:
On a sandstone bluff,
she remains welcoming.
But personally,
her fixed gaze saddens me
as she looks homeward

and sees no angel.
Here she finds me—
a wandering, lost soul—
with her Great-Depression-closed eyes.

Lily of the Nile ("Agapanthus")

Dear Agapanthus lilies,

You stink so bitterly
I can taste you.
And you disrupt
my daydream
in a crowded class
on a sunny afternoon.

Your drought-resistant
purple and white flowers
impress others,
but you make
my head hurt,
though you mean
no harm.

My English teacher
won't let me
get a word in
about you.
Or give me space
for our conversation.
Stop telling me tales
of your tried-and-true life.

While you're outside
enjoying the sea air,
and displaying your
inflorescence,
I'm stuck reading
Great Expectations
and yearning along
with young Pip.

The Earthling

Let's go read
at the old Earthling Bookstore:
The one with the wood stove,
where we could forget
the big move
and the fact that
Miller's Outpost
was so close by.

We're so tired
of expanded
bodies—of shops
turned into megastores,
of stores
turned into malls.
Expanded bodies,
not expanded minds.

And everything
is like everything.
The humming drone
gets louder, and
my experience
is no longer
just mine.

Let's go read
at the old Earthling Bookstore:
The one with the wood stove,
with warm friends
who read banned books,
or write them,
and think for themselves.

Meet Me by the Fig Tree

Meet me by the fig tree.
My mind is in the middle
of a Moreton Bay, Australia romance.

What stories and dreams
are manifest in branches, trunks, and roots
that are well over 100 years old?

The cityscape's giant, too,
had humble origins as a sapling
in Adeline Crabb's nineteenth-century hands.

Was it well worth the voyage
from Eastern Australia to Santa Barbara,
as a gift from Adeline's sailor friend?

Over the twentieth-century years,
it increased its surface area on Montecito Street,
stretching its canopy, claiming its turf—a dead zone for neighbors.

Its grand, pale gray, radiating roots,
luring transients, whinos, and lovers,
have never made peace with other plants.

Maybe it grew and survived for Adeline,
not growing for a perfect beach view,
but rather to see her again.

Meet me by the fig tree.
It's impossible to miss.
Survival is all about living in the meantime.

Bird's Tour

Bop!
The sinewy melody
I play has a
wide, open canvas
with three distant parameters
and my horn can take you there
all in one night.

You'd think we'd start with
the East Coast,
but that is not from where
my music originates.
It comes from the West,
rising up
out of the Camarillo Mental Hospital.

It drives itself up
the Pacific Coast Highway
and loiters with nude bodies
at Gaviota.
Adding to this imagery,
my horn presents to you
pointillistic granules of sand.

In—
This—
Hard—
Groove—
We go—
Up the PCH
to swing with the *Dharma Bums*.

My horn
calls the time.
My horn
is the train.
My horn
is the trip.

From the Cascades
to Seattle,
this night train
becomes quiet,
but scenic,
since it is your first hint
of the seasons.

Pike Place Market,
a view of Elliott Bay.
My horn is a vapor
of freshly made coffee
that warms you
in that glorious moment
in the middle of my fog.
Don't get settled.
For the flight is now happening.
This is the real modulation.
This is beyond tonal implication.
Here we find reminiscence,
and a Dixieland tease.
Let us go dancing in New Orleans.

Louis and King Oliver
are there,
but my horn won't let you forget
Lil Hardin—
Here's a segment of "Just for a Thrill,"
and another from "Oriental Swing."

We've taken ourselves
to the French Market
to admire the artisan's work,
laugh at a young boy's flap ball changes,
correct his sorry riffs,
and fall into his breaks.

As we go to Memphis,
we get innovative by the river
in an imaginary recording studio.
Here is my echo.
Here is my reverb.
Elvis has left the building.

You've seen Chicago
a million times before.
You've got a hint of it
in New Orleans, so . . .
we take ourselves deeper South instead,
walking through Delius' orange groves.

This passage—
Composed here—
Touches the feistiest ocean.
Can't you hear
the cold waves?
I'd give you a colorful animal,
but my horn does not offer goofy images.

This is the Atlantic.
our pace changes as we
exit the Virginia corridor.
We speed past Howard,
and cross the Duke Ellington Bridge,
on the other side,
we meet him, but keep up our pace.

Hot jazz!
I have taken his "Ko-Ko"
as my own and I've hinted at
his "Blue Ramble."
But I must improvise
and my horn must be free.

And just when you believe this song
has become organized,
with a hint of Latin jazz,
my horn flies you
to another destination:
New York.

The heroin's a dream—
The heroin's a scream—
The heroin courses through my veins,
up through my warm breath,
into the horn
and past open keys—
Escapes euphoria,
finding your ears.

Stay with me and my silver spoon.
We'll busker with the Beats,
who don't get my horn,
but like musicians and free spirits
who bring their own demons
to the ceremony.

From nightclub to nightclub,
my horn gives you a snapshot
of heritage, smoke, and
Harlem Renaissance.
The Atlantic turns
this fantasy black and tan.

Another rest in Boston,
then to Vermont and Maine.
To Portland we go
to walk in the sand,
which isn't like the West Coast or the Gulf at all,
is it?

Coda from a horn player:
Morning is here
and it's time to take care
of some unfinished business
about trips to three coasts,
funny drinks,
and your tips.

Pay me well and return tonight.
My horn will be ready
to do the tour another way.
I'll dash my t's and dot my i's
to that promise.
I'll take you there.

Monterey Cypress

Upon a windswept bluff,
contorted branches reach
out to clinch Carmel-by-the-Sea.

The wild waves, sea gulls,
harbor seals, cormorants weave—
a seaside's tapestry.

And from carved granite hills,
extends an oceanic ess:
Here Point Lobos hides its spectacular kelp forests.

There stands a windbreak tree,
sanded down by gusts of sea-blown air.
There stands a windbreak tree,
witnessing your drive to anywhere.

It looks down on its world
from its slanted rocky-coast-formed peak,
taking in denizens of the beach.

Ensnaring, entangling,
branchlets that seek—
the fog belt's apathy.

And north of Big Sur surf,
curtailed by wilderness,
Point Lobos sustains our coastal interests.

There stands a windbreak tree,
sanded down by gusts of sea-blown air.
There stands a windbreak tree,
witnessing your life without a care.

On foot the cameras came
with eyes meant for flat-topped trees.
Apertures open, capturing knotty cypress knees.

Branded by a wildfire blaze,

its helpless scars still try to speak—
of paradise gone so miserably bleak.

And the Pebble Beach golf course
is home to the Lone Cypress
its odd shape holds secrets that old age refuses to confess.

There stands a windbreak tree,
sanded down by gusts of sea-blow air.
There stands a windbreak tree,
witnessing itself as it grows bare.

Summerland Drive

Drive along the curves of the Pacific Coast Highway,
travel south past Montecito on an overcast day.
On your left a yellow house will stand out in your line of view,
On your right you'll see the beach, a tiny cove will guide you.
Enters in your windshield frame the object of your journey:
A stolen glimpse, the "Beach in Pourville," from Monet's Giverny.

Moon Reflection on Goleta Beach, 1986-92

Drive again
on a summer night.
Class is out
and the moon
is shining.
Its reflection
dances on the ocean
to REM
long before
they sang
about Andy.

A walking pier,
near-vacant,
extending, failing
to reach
the horizon
of star-pierced
cobalt sky.

Purple herons
finish off
leftover bait,
enjoying pleasing
one-night stands
with ones
they will love
and ones
they'll leave behind.

The night
is warm enough
not to be
a mere passenger
riding a van
on the PCH
from UCSB
to home.

We have
from 1986
to 1992;
so there's time.

This time,
let's stop.
We never stop.
Let's stop
to walk
that pier,
to see firsthand
that moonlight

We never stop.

Void

It's not here anymore.
You're not here anymore.
It was. It existed. You.
And there it tries to be,
And there we try to make it—
Engaged
in an exchange of nothingness.
Exist now
in blank, negative spaces,
sculptural concepts, visible,
but empty horizons. But not you,
just it. Like it was bound to happen
one day. In fainting,
the slate is blank. In dreams,
I welcome silent space as quiet,
Large scale nothing. This beach—
it might as well be another planet
away from you.

Obsidian Chimes

Hanging from driftwood,
obsidian chimes sound.

Knapped for white snowflakes
and air's harmonic bliss.

The wind makes them ring
their brittle-high tones.

So they leave quietly:
Say goodbye to this muse. . . .

Sinking Sand Bar Mansions

Those fools!
They built
dream houses
on a sand bar.
Didn't they know
like clockwork
they would collapse?

These dream houses,
they might as well
have been built
on the shore,
high-up on faulty stilts.
Or in the fire lane
that burns
to the ground
every twelve years.
Or on mudslide-prone cliffs—
We give that four years.

I guess that enormous,
loaded houses
sink faster
than our homes,
rickety apartments.
And the owners?
Nowhere to be found.
Send the insurance check
to a location undisclosed.
Damn slumlords and
their vacant mess.
All us kids can do
is to go gut them.

Roll up the carpets
before the water
soaks them.
That candelabra?
It's tarnished,
but a Tabasco sauce
cleaning will do.
Someone has gotten to
the chandeliers,
but we'll take
the leftover
crystal tears and beads.
They make
outstanding prisms
and my six-year old cousin
adores them.

The Buildings on a Cliff

And many years later,
the *Daily Nexus*
recalled the death leap
of the lead singer
of the cult band
Penis Brigade
on a bad acid trip.
Nothing is left
of the band's music;
just the playful name.
Too bad
the buildings on a cliff
now tell more
about Isla Vista slumlords,
the town's density being equal
to Calcutta, and
falling drunk frat kids.
What lost potential.

The Bus to The Mesa

Zipped wet suits,
sandy boards,
bare, tarred feet—
A fast bus
heading to
the Mesa,
coasting curves,
winding roads,
swaying left,
swaying right,
suddenly
a swift halt:
This bus ride
always stops
for surfer
nirvana.

Craftsman Bungalow

It is not greedy,
this wonder,
this Berkeley bungalow,
a Bengali innovation,
a celebration,
a many-textured fugue
by Greene & Greene,
enter a short hall,
Burmese teak,
Mahogany wood panels
shipped in
from Honduras,
joined together
with ebony pegs.
The answer by
Frank Lloyd Wright
of leaded glass
cut in tiny squares,
at the door,
a window,
this dwelling
of countless
but now related
materials housed
by a low-pitch
roof line with eaves
and countless
rafters in a matrix,
a woodworker's dream,
a divine fantasy
in local redwood,
that can only end
in a dramatic *stretto*
that features
imitations of
these materials versus
hand woven
wool tapestries
versus metalwork

intertwining copper
and bronze versus
4-over-1
double-hung windows
on the first story
6-over-1
versus gables
and getting plenty
of light and tangible air:
The intensity,
you whisper,
"I want it,"
but it is too precious,
too natural,
too living,
too artistic,
too haunting
to have, but dear,
simple yet
elegant, an
arm's reach
from the beach,
location
an added bonus,
graced by
Japanese bonsai,
the *stretto*,
winds down,
tight, tapered,
hipped-to-
the-hilt formed
with the day's
functional,
decorative
iron brackets,
the ultimate
house
of your dreams.

The Nightmare Tsunami

Fears come true: This long wave train,
forming during falling rain,
targets beach towns sound asleep—
Sevens come to claim their keep.

No one feels the rising tide.
Passing ships, it amplified.
Now it reaches shallow sea.
Cry the birds, "it's time to flee."

What a massive tidal bore,
driving forcefully on shore.
When it smacked its wicked crest,
water flooded homes at rest.

Drawbacks make a sucking sound.
People run to higher ground.
Catch a glimpse of flooded land,
disarray, and displaced sand.

Follow tiny waves called whelps,
bringing forward mangled kelp.
Bodies floating of the dead
leaving all a sense of dread.

Screaming kids strewn far away.
Searching crews begin their day.
Lost a world, but found a shoe.
What? You say you dreamt it, too?

Weimar by the Sea

This is the afterlife
at young Villa Aurora:
Serenus Zeitblom woke up,
staring out the window
of his modern day home
on San Remo Drive
in the Pacific Palisades,
he searches for Wagner,
longing for linden trees.

In these collapsing days,
Bertolt Brecht and he
with severed heritages,
have met with Schoenberg
and an existential sunset:
Expressionist lives
in fragmented shards
plummeting in the sun,
longing for linden trees.

Teddy is too young
to be part of the crowd,
but Serenus has shown him
Adrian's square piano
in return for Schoenberg's
compositional technique,
as close as he'll get
to their closed-off circle,
longing for linden trees.

Far away in Brazil,
north of Rio de Janeiro,
writing after survival,
Zweig could no longer
wake up to defeat;
In a sunnier paradise,
it was all still over,
life became unfulfilling,
longing for linden trees.

Along the Pacific,
pensive Eusebius
with fiery Florestan,
young ghost beach dancers—
Schumann still flickers—
once-upon-a-time culture
a tennis playing composer's vision,
another round with Chaplin,
longing for linden trees.

Is success enough?
Is the cabana enough?
Is the high sun index enough?
Is the mother land enough?
Here Thomas Mann and
his dear Zeitblom wonder,
is life after death enough,
looking out a window,
longing for linden trees.

Fresnel Lens

Aloha, alight,
draw the ships despite weather,
pass on they may
in joint-clipped refrain.

Its multifaceted reflectors
and its vast candlepower,
have captivated us
in their prismatic array.

Aloha, alight,
cleave the dark despite weather,
(un)ravel life may
in joint-clipped refrain.

Its hyper-radial lenses
and its internal reflection
have captivated us
in their prismatic array.

Aloha, alight,
cull the clouds despite weather,
screen them it may
in joint-clipped refrain.

Its concentric rings
and its faceted domes
have captivated us
in their prismatic array.

Aloha, alight,
draw the ships despite weather,
pass on they may
in joint-clipped refrain.

La Monica Ballroom

They're gone:
The hard maple floors
that supported
a premiere ballroom,
a popular dance hall,
Fiddler Spade Cooley's place of operation,
a locale for radio and television broadcasts,
a giant garage
for Jack Benny's weird cars,
a large speed skating rink.
They lasted just one year
after Cooley slammed his wife
Ella Mae Evans' head into a floor
and went to jail for murder.
Gone well before the Beatles' invasion
and the Beach Boys' success.
After all,
a 1920s ballroom turned into
the country and western swing mecca
couldn't support
the awakening progressiveness
of the times,
and therefore
the hard maple floors
that could reveal some histories
must go, too.

Coast Starlight

I smile,
loved, cradled, rocked,
window up against the ocean,
the Cascades,
ravaged nature,
the ocean again.

Seattle's soft water
broken by red construction,
then whitewash
dissolving into Cascades
and four seasons,
ice-dripping rocks,
brown speckled
bright sulfur leaves.

The Starlight route,
moving South through
devouring mountains;
Beat the tracks
into sextuple meter,
a sea shanty splashing
in mild rain.

Announces quietly
Diamond Lake,
Klamath Marsh, then
Klamath Falls—
into deep sleep
and navy noir,
wanting to remember
moments slipped away.

Wake up
to a new route:
The Southern Pacific Coast Daylight
with sun glowing
from California's border
to snow in Mount Shasta,
sleepy Redding,
Chico and the arts
welcome you.

Sacramento,
Davis, driving into
well lectured warm
and evaporating
rice patty fields.
Why bother
to live here
if not on the coast,
Martinez?

Past Suisun
and San Francisco Bays,
the train settles
at Jack London Square
as a passenger
pulls out her
knitting jenny
for a *Call of the Wild*
layover.

Stop and go,
like Steve Jobs
spending limited time
in the Silicon Valley.
A King Fisher greets us
on the way
to spinach fields
in Salinas.
Steinbeck cannot complain
for not being here
anymore.

Sulfur and smokestacks!
The clack of the tracks
echo past Paso Robles,
San Luis Obispo to
Pismo Beach will not
(hopefully)
wake up
that PG&E plant.
Pray for no
aftershocks.

In a distant,
sleepy dream world,
Point Conception:
What an irony.
Cross the damn Tallpass Creek Trestle!
Here is Santa Barbara,
The land of the
open-air bike shop.
Delay: A bum
has thrown a loveseat
on the tracks.

Picking up speed,
from the blue herons
of the Clark Bird Refuge,
along the dried up Ventura River,
in quick succession,
much like the Greyhound Bus:
Ventura, dash Oxnard,
dash Van Nuys.

Van Nuys:
The Coast Starlight
and Pacific Surfliner's
little convenient miracle
of going through the Valley
in lightening speed—
no traffic jam equalizer
and no radio tranquilizer.

The final stretch,
a parallel ride
along the Los Angeles Reservoir,
filled up
with a drop of water
and more gang tags
than the state of Texas.
Homeward, we go.

Here at the homestretch,
we surge forward
and roll backwards
into the station:
Our rocking chariot
looks homeward
and it sees
the City of Angels.

The Japanese Glass Fishing Float

One of many
in a peaceful row,
impressed
by sailor-knotted rope
and years
of overseas voyages.
Its own parents,
a glassblower
and a molten, old Sake bottle.

Catch the light
of the sun,
while floating midair,
imperfect, sand-scraped,
rescued from storms
breaking the circular
California current, fed
way off from
the Northern Pacific,
now a garden ornament.

Up close,
a birthmark,
a raised button seal
with Kanji symbols
revealing a trademark
beyond any purpose
of keeping fishing nets
afloat in the water:
"Maru Toku," Special.

At the Grotto, Fisherman's Wharf, 2007

Rain-beaded taxi ride—
Twilight at Berkeley Marina,
red Golden Gate Bridge sky,
night lights shining on Fisherman's Wharf.

Stumbling past glowing curios shops.
Riding an outdoor merry-go-round
with a meaningless crowd of tourists—
All in a sleepy, astigmatic blur.

Transient comedians and musicians,
a hazy glimpse of wharf entertainment
that leads up to a desired memory: A date
with tuxedoed waiters at the Grotto.

Wet streets and flickering neon signs
of restaurants, now historical landmarks.
The Grotto is open until midnight, still
serving halibut and baked Alaska.

Ground Squirrels at the Berkeley Marina

Eyes peeking between rocks.
Leaps effortlessly between
boats, tiny docks, ropes.
Tail-twitching winks.
These pine seeds,
they're good.

From Ocean Avenue, Santa Monica to Venice West

They came to the ocean,
to settle, to write
just one more time
the Great American novel.

Larry spent his first days
plugging his novels,
rescuing Craig Rice
from fighting this world.

Uppy loved the young couple,
but Rice was his work wife,
whose world crumbled apart
after *Home, Sweet Homicide.*

Postmarks showed changes
from Santa Monica to Venice:
Cheaper rent, but still writing,
beaches change, but still dreaming.

And Larry learned to love
jazz poetry in Venice;
He chronicled these beats
at Venice West Café.

Lectures at UCLA, *Holy Barbarians,*
FREEP, radio scripts, editing poems—
Distractions paid their ocean stay,
the writer typed himself to sleep.

Night came beats and bongos,
sound recordings, performance happenings;
To Rexroth he bragged about
his discovered "Slum by the Sea."

No matter how hard he tried,
he couldn't drum up the business,
he couldn't edit the poems enough
to capture the world's attention.

An editor, a chronicler,
accused of over-playing his cards
selling Venice's fleeting poetry,
preserving it all anyway.

He saved a wild Perkoff,
who wrote an elegy to Bird,
suggesting refined words
and timing in red crayon.

So he and wife Nettie,
in their "Slum by the Sea,"
kept hope alive for dear Bruno,
burned at the stake for his art.

He continued to pursue
the Great American novel,
leaving the world with his dreams
still alive for scholars to find.

Harry Partch's Shipyard

A mid-century exploration,
touching stars on still nights long
before the inevitable moon landing
or petite, white musical men
in status-quo navy pinstripe suits
took up studying him for promotions.

An abandoned shipyard in Sausalito,
whereabouts of Harry Partch,
instrument builder for his own music,
belonging to his own belonging,
belonging to the classicals,
belonging to the populars,
like the madrigal puts it,
in the end, convening alone
with Castor and Pollux.

Neither the first place nor the last
place the hobo composer settled
to dream of his microtonal world
and instruments meant to live,
not be stored in a museum—
breathe Surrogate Kithara,
Harmonic Canon II from
Harmonic Canon I's base,
Kithara II and Boo I
in tantalizing Sausalito air.

In Sausalito, like great ships,
the instruments have gone
to join the greater workings of dances,
calluses required for the bright
Surrogate Kithara's green and orange hexads,
while Harmonic Canon II mirrors
Castor (left) and Pollux (right)—
non-identical twins, each 44 strings;
Boo I, the bamboo marimba,
requires its tongues to be tuned.

Phrases and moon phases
must repeat frequently,
and Partch knew well
that familiarity grows
with all created themes—
his stars found single and double
exposures, emitted by wood,
Plexiglas, and second guitar strings,
bamboo percussion,
folk like rhythmic alternations,
and lonely, innovative mind works.

Buskers at Dusk

Just before
bulldozers
come to clear
dead winos,
wafts another
round softly
of "Purple Haze,"

Rollo not
Rollo blunt
sings his way
of sunny blues
of Sonny's blues.

Trash can fires
lit by cheap
tequila
keep the songs
still coming
with bangs from
glass marbles
in white plastic
paint containers,
ancestors of
the bongos,
here long before
selfish passersby
who believe a
street artist
should never
be paid.

Third Street Promenade

A slow errand stroll
with a break,
ticking down seventy-degree-weather time
with an Orange Julius:
The kind made with raw egg.

Things to do
in pre-topiary and gentrified dinosaur time
took place shoulder-to-shoulder
with famous giants who also loved the beach.

Hit the sales at Europa
and ran into Red Skeleton
gathering remnants at the silk shop.
We had just seen him at the post office.

Window-shop,
staring at the pink rhinestone thistle
at an undisclosed, quaint Scottish store,
where Eva Gabor just bought a tartan scarf.

The sleepy morning
continued at a health store
where pre-juicing Jack LaLanne and his wife
sold sesame bars to die for.

Up to Woolworth's
to say hello
to Roald Dahl, Patricia Neal, and Vincent Price,
who don't mind babysitting me for a moment.

As we left,
Paul Newman and his security guard
greeted us at the crosswalk,
catching Gloria Swanson's giant pink-bowed hat.

Final Night at Palisades Park, 2008

October-purple clouds and moonlit-black Pacific,
brought on by Santa Ana winds and a perfect evening out.

I walk alone from Broadway to Palisades Park,
looking beyond the Sunset Trail to that something eternal.

St. Monica stands quietly praying to her city
while I'm fulfilling my curiosity of seeing her at night.

Hell, if I had only known it was your last night in Santa Monica,
I would have invited you to walk with me.

Longboards on Stearns Wharf

Pictures return thoughts
of a sunny afternoon
sitting at Longboards,
eating a simple meal
that was just a dream
when we were young.

Pigeons fly in, flood
the open deck:
Multicolored flying rats
requesting scraps,
daring to jump onto
whine tasters' tables,
rail-tiptoeing towards
the ultimate end—
A beautiful panorama
of sun-shimmered
surf at East Beach.

Santa Barbara Light

Twilight, a starburst,
a fake lighthouse, a beacon,
where we catch the bus.

Wrack Zone

This wrack zone
forming in some vicinity
of Julia Child's condo
consists of deposits
of driftwood—
of brown kelp—
of pier pilings—
of garbage—
of my thoughts—
and accumulated bygone
waves that leave their treads
on the sea strand.

Two globetrotting plovers,
Who have returned
From the five and dime,
perhaps Boston,
or Paris:
One tall and stately,
the other less so,
but still sweet and soft,
pitter-patter across
broken driftwood,
admiring trinkets,
mulling over tokens,
and still in love
enough
to flirt—
to kiss—
on a marine junkyard,
the coastal terrace
of their Montecito dreams.

Ficus

Oh, Benjamin,
droop branchlets
of glossy leaves.
Weep figs,
bird offerings,
crunchy, immature fruit.
Tell ancient tales
of invading gardens,
finding office space,
and rapidly becoming
that stately tree
in whitewashed days,
shading a bus stop
while lifting up
concrete sidewalks.

Kenneth Rexroth's Place of Rest

The pepper trees blossom red at UCSB,
where your lectures, long passed, linger on
in riffs of thought, wandering the lagoon.

In your time, the world was too insulting
for your intelligence, for wisdom to grasp
was an art you mastered just before your prime.

And your words still dance like your swan, who
sings in your honor at the nearby bird refuge, or
in the minds of smiling ears of jazz enthusiasts.

Out West, here in Santa Barbara, a home
for your poems, interweaving with music and nature,
mixing in your humorous wit among grown-up children.

Homages and thoughtful words stretch beyond
Channel Drive, beyond the Biltmore, beyond
Music Academy of the West's crisscross gazebo.

Asleep, facing the ocean, open poems and re-read
essays, dreams iconoclast still, in opposite direction,
appropriately against the main stream of sleeping neighbors.

World Pacific Records

Sound it before that damned "Elusive Butterfly."
Sound it with Chet, Gerry, Desmond, and Chico.
Sound it with experimental instruments, jazz cello by Katz.
Sound it before the days when Liberty bought it,
before the days of the Ventures and their hits.

Drop the needle on quintets in High-Fi,
let it crackle, indestructible broad canvas capturing
the ch, ch-ch-ch whispers of hanging cymbals,
the dotted rhythms of a French horn running out of air.
You didn't know that L.A. once had it so together.

Bloop

Hail,
underwater,
ultra-low frequency,
unexplained
BLOOP.

Are you
a siren's love call
for Cthulhu?
An ice quake?
An iceberg
scraping
the ocean floor?

You're inhuman.

Since the '90s,
NOAA wants
to know
all about you.

Their want ad
also questions
the whereabouts
of Julia, Train,
Slow Down,
Whistle, and Upsweep.

Homeopath's Tea House

We didn't know the password,
but they let us stay anyways,
besides, we were fascinated
by the blue cohosh, the verbena,
and the "Mystic Mint."

A bright-eyed doctor
nicknamed "Medusa Head"
smiled at us as he applied
Golden Seal to his mouth sores
and looked at a mirror.

"That ocean breeze is a menace
to your teeth and voice."
The yellow-toothed doctor
pointed to wads of dried kelp
and chopped bits of ginger.

"Are you from here?"
We are on our best days.
Returning to our admiration
of red apothecary drawers,
we hesitated to make a selection.

We stayed and listened to waves,
drank from our magical
iron Tetsubin made for two,
taking in medicinal powers
of the tea called "Mystic Mint."

An hour later, we ordered some Szechuan takeout.

Ashes

Not "at,"
but "with"—
Lost *with* sea.

It's mostly
a firm choice,
to be forever-stirred
in Pacific Ocean
waves and whirls,
drifting to someday
being reduced
to no words.

Spiral

Live vicariously through me?
You're a parental parasite. I
read every life chapter, turning
chamber after chamber in
ammonite revolutions,
a frustrating segment of time,
time—I win—time running out,
completing the book about
what I should have been.

Brand New Beach Mat

My brand new beach mat
of goldenrod straw
is lined with
turquoise cotton edging.

I bought it from Europa,
that little sheet store
on the Third Street Promenade,
on my way to the beach.

It was rolled up and tied
along with other beach mats
on sale—a festive arrangement
of clearance items.

The new beach mat
looks good here
next to my box
of crackers and towels.

I have become part
of a beach blanket film,
creating a scene
too perfect to forget.

If nobody steps on it,
tosses sand on it,
or steals it while I'm wading,
it will still be new.

Whatever its fate,
I want to take it home,
hang it off a curtain rod,
and turn it into a shade.

Following The Sunrays

So, this is where it all began,
chasing The Sunrays, a band,
who opened for The Beach Boys,
and singing their hit "Andrea."

These were the vacant beach bluff days
when band mates like Eddy Medora
switched out their 1950s saxophone
for surfer guitar, electric and amplified.

Stripping their Dirt Riders and Renegades image,
they opted to be managed by Wilsons's dad,
and the die-hard fans argued to their graves:
The Sunrays were ripped off.

Travel in time up the PCH
to find a joyous beach-sun ritual
with leather jackets and Hawaiian shirts
flailing hands in the sky to hear "Still."

In these days, *Gidget's* California was real,
The Sunrays played for the kids,
Professor Lawrence lectured at UCLA,
and they had a special understanding.

They played at the Crescendo Interlude,
a Sunset Strip venue, named appropriately,
a contrast to the Pacific Ocean Park
and their excited teenage crowds.

These were the days The Sunrays
would share the stage with "Peppermint Twist"
Joey Dee and the Starliters, responding
with "Outta Gas" and "Car Party."

Weekends were spent as good times,
following The Sunrays venue to venue,
maybe as far as San Bernardino, away
from the ocean, the surfers, the sand.

These days, they're photos, fading stories,
rare good times in busy students' lives.
Their songs a release, a bright reminder
that in this life, the sun is obliviously happy.

Following The Sunrays, they reached, hands
outstretched to receive a transmission:
ethereal, musical, dancing, joyous light,
"Don't Worry Baby," "I Live for the Sun."

Sea Glass

Soft abrasions,
worn from straight lines
to impossible smooth curves.

No longer sharp shards.
No longer containers.

The world that was yours
Doesn't exist anymore.

Westward Ho and Gone

In a past life of mine,
Miriam Janucek skated fearlessly
down Armacost Avenue to National,
making her way to the Westward Ho Supermarket
in her metal roller skates
that locked onto her tennis shoes.

She was just a smart little girl
who wanted to escape
her conservative Jewish mother
and her strict ways
to go and live with her sweet
Czechoslovakian father,
who meant the world to her.
She never did it.

I had plans to run away, too.
Being just eight, I'd have to wait a while,
but every morning for nearly a year,
I'd open the door before my parents woke,
and I'd run down the cul-de-sac, turn the corner
at the stop sign, and dart up that same street,
as fast as I could until that guilty voice
made me go home.

I couldn't leave my mom alone with him.

But for the same amount of time,
I became a nobody to them.
I was kicked out of my mom's favorite school.
My parents lied about our address—
I don't know who told on us,
but it was my fault,
and I was tired of spending time
with an old black and white TV
watching *Twilight Zone* marathons,
Woody Woodpecker, and *The Little Rascals*.

I was tired of bruiseless slaps,
of cursing chases around the oak coffee table,
and waiting forever
for my mother to get it together,
so we could just leave.
I had a plan,
and she was allocated limited time
to get over her unreasonable frustration
that seemed too long for me to stand.

It made sense to run down the street,
knowing one day
I'd get to the Westward Ho market,
perhaps on my own ball bearings
rather than as an anxiety-driven escape.

I'd sleep in a mall store at night
go to school during the day,
spend free time at the Santa Monica Pier.
I knew there was no circus in L.A., so
somehow, I'd make money, steal food,
shoplift school supplies and lip gloss.
Most importantly, I'd find my peace.

But I couldn't leave my mom alone with him.

When Motel 6 Was Our Home

I was a wild child,
picking pockets
to support my escape plan,
coloring Shrinky Dinks,
fantasizing the day of their baking.

I was still pissed off
for giving up everything
to go into hiding,
and friends;
I told them we were moving to Buenos Aires.

A warm, clean room:
A fresh and modern start
to a battered mother
and abused child on the run,
a school with two luxurious queen beds.

San Roque, Almost Equidistant to the Beaches

A little old lady land,
the "nearly dead" counterpart
to Santa Barbara's "newly wed,"
San Roque lies
almost equidistant to the beaches.
But nobody bothers
to check that fact.
It just is, and in January
it's lined with snowcaps
behind Mediterranean foothills.
That and its topiary masterpieces
make it resemble a Japanese village
peppered with star pines, baby bottle brushes,
and ficuses.

On one of several cul de sacs
a little apartment complex
known as Las Brisas
hinted at the paradise
with its teak-like wood overpasses
and fences wrapped in thin bamboo.
A redwood tree
that still stands today
marks where we kids
had made our forts.

Angel the Chihuahua
and her sweet
granny-circle making owner,
the Danish baker,
not to mention the lovely Mr. Riddle,
have left the world long ago.
We were the grandchildren
they were meant to have.
And unlike that mean, crazy man
who lived down the street,
they let us take their wood scraps.

Star Pines

If you come to Santa Barbara by train,
star pines and rainbow flags
form the greeting landscape.

If you sit down to take a break,
look up into the trees
and you'll find the aligning stars.

Soft needles bring you near,
connecting you from Hollywood to Haifa,
to the Big Dogs beachside shop across the street,
to stars four and more feet above your head
that are actually millions of light years away.

The Singing Sand

Silence, like a *Laurence of Arabia* sound image:
Wind shearing sand,
soft layer by layer.
An excerpt of *Desert Music* plays
in the middle of nowhere,
as we aim to visit
the Colossi of Memnon,
which was really just a mirage-oasis
created by Kafka idealists
who couldn't stand
being beaten down by the sun.
Don't go where ledges are sand:
Hundred-foot drops are created
by the shuffles of small, thong-bearing feet.
Roars, whistles, and booms,
the song of the dunes
in squawks vicariously living through thin air—
You are not to cause any friction here.
Light. After light. After light. After
rows of cars ignoring singing sand,
traveling down dead garnet roads.
Oblivious to singing oblivion,
car lights on in the middle of the day
are just a clear sign
that Peter Sellers must have died.
And the sand doesn't hesitate to begin
its raspy whisper-lament:
"This is the Symphony
that Schubert wrote
and never finished."

Turquoise

The Pacific Ocean waves incessantly
its bright turquoise and white wash.

Its calm name must exist only in that one color
that belongs to no other ocean in the world.

The waves bring memory, grief, greetings—
They change roles, depending on the moon.

At night on the water is a variety
of glimmering creature reflections.

Which one are you?
Sea Monster? Disappearing seagull?

You can sleep all day, sleep through your life,
and the turquoise waves never cease.

They stir the ashes and sand,
fixing by perpetually unfixing its slurry.

On the murkiest, foggiest, choppiest days,
the turquoise forever remains.

Drive your car over the edge of the road,
and that turquoise will welcome you.

Dare to walk on water, drown your sorrows,
and it will engulf you as if it were starving.

Sometimes, the Pacific picks its own fragments,
drags them under, and permanently claims them.

Turquoise is also a bright day surfing
or just blue flirting with becoming green.

Simple eye contact with the turquoise
connects you to artists, musicians, and writers long gone.

There are many others,
but I prefer greeting Patchen, Rexroth, Mingus, Parker.

Lipton, who meant to write
his Great American Novel.

And Miles, who straddled jazz styles
to compose wild, beautiful turquoise fusion:

A horn player's echo down a sinewy road running
parallel to the ocean's coolness, a coast located on your left.

NOTES

In the process of writing several poems, I did research and consulted sources listed here, organized by poem title.

My Diebenkorn World

Quotation of Diebenkorn curator Sarah Bancroft, describing the artist painting in "riotous calm," by Susan Stamberg, "In 'Ocean Park,' Gentle Portraits of California Light." *NPR*. 2 March 2012. http://www.npr.org/2012/03/02/147722483/in-ocean-park-gentle-portraits-of-california-light. Accessed on 12 March 2015.

Red Tide

The poem plays on Wallace Stevens's "Disillusionment of Ten O'Clock," in his *Harmonium* (New York: Alfred A. Knopf, 1923).

The Shark Purse

This poem plays on Marc Blitzstein's 1954 translation of "Die Moritat von Mackie Messer" from the drama *Die Dreigroschenoper* (1928) with music by Kurt Weill and text by Bertolt Brecht. My source recording was by Louis Armstrong and His All-Stars (1956, Coronet, KS-349).

Weimar by the Sea

The idea of a poem about Thomas Mann, his characters Serenus Zeitblom and Adrian Leverkühn, Arnold Schonberg's circle, and contemporaries settling in California, in addition to Stefan Zweig, came to me while reading Thomas Mann, *Doctor Faustus: The Life of the German Composer Adrian Leverkühn as Told by a Friend*, trans. John E. Woods (New York: Vintage Books, 1999), 354, 356 ("days of collapse and capitulation . . ."), and 474 ("Everything is pushing and plummeting toward the end . . . ").

Harry Partch's Shipyard

Research on Partch's instruments and works includes his essay, "The Rhythmic Motivations of *Castor and Pollux* and *Even Wild Horses*: 1952," in Harry Partch, *Bitter Music: Collected Journals, Essays, Introductions, and Librettos*, 1st paperback ed., ed. Thomas McGeary (Urbana and Chicago: University of Illinois Press, 2000), 224-25, as well as Partch's "String and Voice Instruments" and "Percussion Instruments," in *Genesis of a*

Music: An Account of a Creative Work, Its Roots and Its Fulfillments, 2d ed. (New York: Da Capo Press, 1974), 231-35 and 242-44 (Surrogate Kithara and Harmonic Canon II), and 282-85 (Boo I). The idea about "classicals" and "populars" mentioned in the poem alludes to Partch's discussion about to which composers' classification or group he belongs. See Partch, "The Rhythmic Motivations of *Castor and Pollux* and *Even Wild Horses*: 1952," in *Bitter Music*, 221-22.

www.ingramcontent.com/pod-product-compliance
Lightning Source LLC
Chambersburg PA
CBHW020858090426
42736CB00008B/422